# MOVE FAST

# MOVE FAST

## HOW **FACEBOOK** BUILDS SOFTWARE

### JEFF MEYERSON

MOVE FAST

*How Facebook Builds Software*

ISBN   978-1-5445-1755-1 *Hardcover*

   978-1-5445-1754-4 *Paperback*

   978-1-5445-1753-7 *Ebook*

*For my parents, Gayle Rosenthal and Robert Meyerson.*

# CONTENTS

# FOREWORD

Move fast and break things.

Today, Facebook's infamous engineering motto is almost universally derided, but back when I first set foot in the now-demolished Facebook office at 1601 California Ave. for my interview as a new grad in 2010, it meant something different. It was exciting. Ambitious. Motivating. And certainly provocative.

My mother had just seen *The Social Network* and offered her judgement: "You shouldn't work for that Mark Zuckerberg; he doesn't seem like a very nice boy."

After leaving the company to found a startup that was later acquired by Twitter (where I work today), I started to realize that Facebook Engineering operated quite differently from any other organization. This difference gave the company a number of unique advantages that directly contributed to its once-in-a-generation success.

To me, it was crazy that the world knew so much about how other great companies like Google, Amazon, and Spotify built software but knew so little of Facebook's engineering culture and practices. I thought this was a story that needed to be told, and when I bounced the idea off of my good friend and former Facebooker Nick Schrock, he enthusiastically agreed. We joined forces with Jeff Meyerson of Software Engineering Daily to do a series of podcast episodes with prominent Facebook Engineering leaders from our era.

The interviews were so good that we decided to evolve them into this book.

This book focuses on 2011-2014, a critical moment in the company's history. During this three-year period, Facebook went through enormous change. It went public, pivoted the entire company to mobile, defeated Google+, and made three of its most consequential acquisitions: Instagram, WhatsApp and Oculus.

Accomplishing all of this in such a short period of time required an engineering organization that could deliver at the highest level.

This book takes a decidedly engineering-centric point of view. Regardless of how you feel about the company, Mark Zuckerberg, or the impact of social media on the world, it's undeniable that Facebook is an execution machine and one of the most successful startups of all time. Facebook Engineering enabled that execution and had to rethink many engineering best practices in order to rise to the challenge.

This is not a book about policy nor about the impact of policies on society. This is a book about execution. Even Facebook's fiercest critics do not deny its ability to relentlessly execute on its engineering objectives.

While the Facebook Engineering playbook won't work for everyone, it does offer an alternative perspective and a fresh look at many so-called best practices. I hope you enjoy getting to meet the motley crew that built Facebook during one of its most transformative periods and can take some of the lessons back to your own engineering organization.

—PETE HUNT

# INTRODUCTION

*"The whole 'move fast and break things' motto is misunderstood. It's subtle, and people don't like subtlety."*

—MIKE VERNAL, FORMER FACEBOOK EXECUTIVE

## MOVE FAST

The pace of change is accelerating.

Mobile computing emerged in 2007 with the creation of the iPhone and made humans constantly connected to each other. Cloud computing lowered the capital expense of starting a software product to $0, which has led to a boom in new technology companies. Social media has changed how communities are formed, and how decisions are made.

Mobile, cloud, and social media are software trends with powerful momentum. The world is changing quickly, and in this environment, the only way for a business to stay relevant is to move fast.

"Move fast and break things" was articulated by Facebook CEO Mark Zuckerberg in the early years of the company. Facebook needed to build new features faster than MySpace in order to take the market. By 2014, Facebook had earned a commanding lead in the social networking category. The phrase was updated to, "Move fast with stable infrastructure."

It is easy to see why Facebook moves fast. This book is about how they do it and how you can apply the principles of moving fast to your own business or creative project.

Over the last fifteen years, Facebook has changed every major aspect of our lives. Childhood, dating, politics, food, business, and music are all different from how they were before Facebook. The software we use defines our lives, and Facebook creates much of that software.

We all know that Facebook has changed our lives, and we know that it will continue to change our lives in the coming years. But we don't know what is coming next. The consequences of Facebook's decisions are impossible to predict, even for the company itself.

You may not like Facebook. But you cannot deny its impact.

All that said, this book is not a comprehensive story about Facebook's history. This book is about strategy—specifically the strategies that Facebook has used to build software that has had an impact. More generally, it is a book about how a software company can think about strategy and how to implement that strategy through products, culture, and technology.

## WHY THIS BOOK EXISTS

I host a podcast called *Software Daily*. We produce a sixty-minute show every weekday. Each episode is an interview with a software industry professional.

Over the last five years, *Software Daily* has featured more than 1,000 interviews with engineers, CEOs, managers, investors, and industry analysts. Topics have included cloud computing, databases, and business strategy.

A year ago, I started having conversations with two former Facebook engineers, Pete Hunt and Nick Schrock. Pete and Nick had spent their early careers at Facebook, and were at that time leading engineering teams outside of the company. They were finding that many of Facebook's best engineering practices were unknown to the broader industry.

Pete and Nick were convinced that if the outside world knew about how Facebook engineering worked, many companies would benefit from that knowledge. I was curious myself, so I began interviewing engineers from Facebook on *Software Daily*.

Like many other people at the time, I believed that Facebook's engineering culture was largely a copy of Google's. But Facebook and Google work very differently.

Over the course of more than twenty-five interviews with Facebook engineers, product managers, and executives, I discovered that Facebook engineering is as unique as the product itself.

Facebook's engineering organization is built for speed. Products are created quickly. Engineers build tools to support the fast pace of product creation. The entire culture of Facebook is structured to select for people who thrive in a fast environment. And everyone knows that the excess of speed has caused problems for Facebook from time-to-time.

For better and worse, moving fast has greatly differentiated Facebook's execution.

Pete and Nick were correct: there are many untold stories within Facebook engineering. After conducting my interviews with current and former Facebook engineers, a set of ideas emerged that we felt would be useful to the business community.

## CASE STUDY

The book is divided into three parts: Product, Culture, and Technology.

The first section is about Facebook's product strategy. Facebook has always been a social networking company, but in 2011 it was forced to become a mobile company. The change in consumer preferences towards mobile phones was an existential threat to Facebook. We start the book by exploring how Facebook maneuvered the entire organization through a platform shift that could have killed the company. We also consider Facebook's strategic response to Google+.

Facebook's product strategy is closely tied to its culture, and culture is the second focal point of the book. The Facebook product needs to continually shift in response to changing consumer preferences, and the Facebook culture supports this constant evolution. Employees are encouraged to pursue their individual career goals, and this emphasis on individuality is in productive tension with the strongly cohesive company culture.

Facebook has a program called bootcamp which provides the organization's cultural backbone. Bootcamp is the onboarding process for new Facebook employees, and as these employees go through bootcamp they are given freedom to choose what part of the organization they end up joining.

The third section of the book is about Facebook's technology stack. Facebook engineering has been shaped by the business problems that the company has solved. Facebook was built before cloud computing and SaaS products, so it has had to build a wide range of tools in-house.

Engineers within Facebook build the products that make Facebook money, and they build internal tools that make the product development process more efficient. Pivoting to mobile forced Facebook to develop new systems for networking and release management. Frontend performance problems led to the creation of ReactJS, and backend performance problems led to the creation of the HHVM toolchain to improve PHP execution.

Throughout the different sections of the book, we hope to paint a holistic picture of how Facebook builds software, and why the company moves fast.

Moving fast provides Facebook with numerous benefits. A faster iteration cycle causes products to rapidly improve. Hypotheses can be tested more quickly. The best employees will be more likely to stick with a fast moving company, because they don't get bored. Facebook is a case study in how a company can operate productively in an environment of rapid change. The world is changing fast, so Facebook moves fast.

Although Facebook is a unique company, there are lessons that we can take away from its success. Every company can adopt a strategy that benefits from our world's rapid pace of change, rather than suffering from it.

This book is not prescriptive about how software should be built. The goal is to offer the reader information and strategies based on how Facebook builds software. For more details, including the twenty-five podcast interviews with Facebook engineers that form the basis for this show, you can visit SoftwareDaily.com, subscribe to the *Software Daily* podcast, or download the Software Daily apps for iOS or Android.

# PART 1

# PRODUCT

# PIVOT

*"The biggest mistake we made as a company was betting too much on HTML5 as opposed to native."*

—MARK ZUCKERBERG, 2012

In my interviews with Facebook engineers, one story repeatedly came up: the pivot to mobile.

Facebook was started in 2004, before the iPhone was released, and the iPhone changed everything for consumer applications. Facebook has had many crises in its history, but the most dangerous moment was the shift in consumer trends towards mobile device usage.

Many companies go through this kind of moment: an existential threat that might destroy the profit center or ruin the company culture. Some companies die during this moment, unable to make the proper adjustments. The companies who survive tend to come out of the crisis with renewed strength and momentum.

The rise of mobile devices threatened to kill Facebook. By responding quickly, Facebook turned mobile into its largest source of revenue.

The iPhone was released in 2007. At the time, Facebook was three years old, valued at $15 billion, and was used as a desktop web application. Users would log on to Facebook.com after school or work, and spend hours looking at each other's profiles, posting status updates, and sending messages to each other.

When the iPhone came out, it was not obvious how much of an impact the advent of mobile computing would have on Facebook. Even through 2009, Facebook usage was mostly on the desktop browser. Facebook had 360 million users at the time, the vast majority of whom accessed Facebook from the desktop rather than a mobile device.

By 2010, Facebook's software development team comprised more than 300 engineers. Few of those engineers had expertise in mobile software. Facebook had only made small initial investments into supporting smartphone users, because the mobile user base was so small. The team wanted to make sure that an iPhone user could open a mobile browser and go to Facebook.com over a cellular network, but there was no expectation that mobile computing would be crucial to Facebook.

Throughout 2010, Facebook started to see an increase in the number of logins on mobile. The data suggested that the smartphone was rising in importance, and Facebook did not have a high-quality mobile experience.

With smartphone adoption growing, Facebook started to take mobile seriously in 2010. The first significant effort at mobile was based on HTML5, a technology that would give the company the dynamic, fast product iteration speed that Facebook had developed as a desktop web application.

A solution built around HTML5 would let Facebook centralize its mobile efforts on a single programming language, rather than writing one application in Objective-C for iOS and another in Java for Android.

Unfortunately for Facebook, HTML5 apps were very slow. Facebook soon realized that the HTML5 application was not performing as well as applications built in native iOS and Android code. HTML5 mobile performance was sluggish and choppy. HTML5 applications were also unable to integrate closely with the camera, accelerometer, and other hardware features.

By 2010, Facebook was an organization of hundreds of

people, and most employees did not realize how acute the mobile problem was. But in the engineering department, Facebook's mobile experience was a growing concern.

Mike Vernal is a bookish, tactical executive who worked at Microsoft before joining Facebook in 2008. Today, Mike works as an investor at the storied venture capital firm Sequoia Capital. As an investor, his decision framework is heavily influenced by the lessons of success and failure that he learned over his fourteen years as an engineer and manager.

Before joining Facebook, Mike was used to the product development cadence of Microsoft, which often involved large, bureaucratic teams.

His transition to the fast environment of Facebook was initially a culture shock for Mike. When he joined, there were only seventy engineers at the entire company, compared to his past life at Microsoft where hundreds of engineers might be working on a single product.

Mike's first project at Facebook was Facebook Login, a system for using Facebook to log in to third-party applications throughout the Internet. Despite the complexity of this product, Mike and two other engineers built Facebook Login in just four months. "The implementation was either ingenious or hacky, depending on your disposition," says Mike.

With Facebook Login, Mike saw that a small team motivated by a sense of urgency and opportunity was able to produce something that might not have been attainable by a much larger team. Facebook Login was released quickly and then improved quickly, in a product development strategy Facebook has applied throughout its history.

"There are a bunch of pros and cons to 'move fast and break things,'" says Mike. "It increases the tempo within the engineering org. You become willing to accept a few mistakes in the interest of making the codebase better, faster, and stronger. It was definitional for Facebook."

By 2011, Mike was a Facebook executive in charge of engineering and product strategy. He managed several teams who were planning product demos for the Facebook F8 conference, which is held every year to announce Facebook's new software and vision for the future. The planned product demos were all browser-based desktop computing experiences.

Mike describes the 2011 F8 conference as the moment when reality caught up to Facebook: mobile was changing the consumer Internet, and Facebook was not prepared for that shift.

During F8 2011, Facebook announced new products for digital music, social gaming, and marketing. But none of these features would matter if Facebook did not have a usable mobile application.

"We realized we had been distracted for nine months," Mike says. "We shipped a bunch of stuff that was entirely desktop-centric." Mobile had seemed small at first, and Facebook had not taken it seriously enough. By 2011, it was clear that consumers were shifting their usage, and Facebook had to restructure its entire product development process around mobile computing.

Facebook's HTML5 strategy for mobile computing had been done in the spirit of moving fast. A uniform HTML5 app together with the LAMP backend stack allowed Facebook to iterate on mobile as quickly as it had on the web.

But HTML5 was slow. And Facebook could not simply build on top of HTML5 and fix performance issues over time with iteration. Applications written in HTML5 could not take advantage of the iOS and Android APIs that were available to developers writing native code. HTML5 was fundamentally worse.

In order to build high-quality mobile applications, Facebook would need to start from scratch and go entirely native.

As Facebook started to rebuild its iOS and Android apps, Jocelyn Goldfein was working on the mobile engineering effort. Jocelyn has curly hair and a bubbly personality, but as she recalls the difficult mobile engineering process, her brow furrows with a war veteran's reminiscence. The brightly lit office that I interviewed her in seemed to get dimmer as she began to discuss the journey to native mobile applications.

"HTML5 had been a nine-month wrong turn. We acknowledged that we needed to go native."

As Facebook began to pivot to mobile, its biggest problem was its lack of mobile engineers. Facebook had been built on the web, and web engineers do not have the skills necessary to build native mobile applications.

Facebook started recruiting mobile engineers as fast as possible. The hiring push was so aggressive that Facebook was acquiring small companies just so that they could bring in the necessary mobile talent, a strategy known as acqui-hiring.

"We made massive alterations to how we recruit and interview, all with the intention of being mobile first," says Jocelyn. After a focused sprint of hiring, Facebook now had a core group of twenty people who knew how to build for mobile. "They were heroic. They started to build really good Apple and Android native applications."

To increase the size of the mobile team, Facebook encouraged web engineers who had been at the company for a long time to start learning mobile. Two-week classes were created to retrain web engineers as mobile engineers.

As the mobile engineering efforts grew larger, the mobile development process began to clash with the web development process. Web developers wanted to release new products and move quickly, but mobile developers needed to move at a slower pace.

The web engineers felt constrained, because products need to be released on the web at the same time they are released on mobile. A user expects their mobile application experience to have the same features that are available on the web. Consequently, product development can only move as fast as the slowest team. And at Facebook, mobile was moving considerably slower than web.

Why is mobile application development so much slower than web development? The simplest answer is that there is a manual review process for every mobile app released to the Google Play or Apple App store. In both the Apple and Google review process, a new application version must be submitted to be manually tested for bugs and usability problems.

This app store review process sharply contrasts with web development, where new application versions are deployed to the Internet without the oversight of a human reviewer. Developers can go from idea to website without any intervention.

The native app review process slows down development significantly. Facebook found its tendency to move fast blocked by the delays of app store review.

Facebook engineers who were used to web development were perplexed by the mobile release process. They wondered why it needed to be so much slower than traditional web development, where a change to PHP and HTML could be instantly delivered to the user.

The difference in speed between mobile and web engineers at Facebook was worsened by the fact that a large portion of the mobile team had come from other companies. These mobile engineers were not used to the fast pace of Facebook. They were used to releasing every eight weeks, rather than every day.

In the world of mobile, such a slow release cycle is normal. It allows for a consistent workflow that accounts for the large delays due to app store review.

Facebook engineers had built their skills on the web, where errors are much easier to fix. Facebook engineers were used to shipping products out rapidly, seeing their results live, and iterating on the outcomes. When Facebook engineers were forced to move at the slow pace of mobile development, they felt that something was inherently wrong in the overall process.

The cultural gap between Facebook's web and mobile engineers created tensions within the company. "They came from these very different backgrounds," says Jocelyn. "They were just talking past each other. The mobile apps had to run on eight-week release cycles, Facebook web developers wanted to move faster. The mobile engineers identified themselves as the gatekeepers against the barbarian Facebook product engineers."

Although Facebook's mobile development process was messy, the overall strategy was successful: the native mobile apps improved, and users started to engage with Facebook on mobile with the same ferocity as Facebook had originally been used on the web. "Only took four years," says Jocelyn ruefully. "Facebook was good at turning on a dime. But the mobile pivot was more like turning on a truckload of dimes."

Facebook was not alone in feeling the pain of the platform shift to mobile.

Across the tech industry, the frictions between web and mobile development were straining engineering resources and causing widespread low-quality user experiences. Every company was struggling to figure out how to resolve the discord among engineering teams, and nobody knew exactly how to find harmony across Android, iOS and web.

There was no easy solution. Android is owned by Google. iOS is owned by Apple. Facebook could not change the nature of mobile development. The best option was to create structures within the company that would allow Facebook to work around the inherent difficulties.

Facebook focused all of its resources to make the pivot to mobile. The company changed its practices around hiring, culture, and product development.

Now that Facebook had moved past the moment of existential crisis, the company needed a structure that allowed it to get back to thinking about building new products that met the additional requirements of mobile.

To sustain its mobile quality, Facebook reorganized its mobile engineers. A centralized mobile infrastructure team was formed to build frameworks for performance tooling, quality measurement, and release management. In addition, mobile engineers were assigned to teams for individual features such as Groups, Events, and Messenger.

The central mobile infrastructure team supported aspects

of mobile development that stretched across the company, and the mobile engineers who worked on feature teams worked on the individual minutiae of those mobile features.

After the company pivoted its resources to mobile, the Facebook app became tremendously popular. By 2013, Facebook's mobile ad revenue passed $2 billion and was growing quickly. Today, thanks to its success on mobile, Facebook now has a highly profitable business model of advertising to users on the Facebook app.

As of August 2019, 96 percent of Facebook users access the site through a mobile device. Facebook's most recent earnings in 2019 were $16.9 billion. Ninety-four percent of those earnings came from advertising on mobile devices. The platform that initially caused a crisis for Facebook has become the primary source of revenue for the company.

Mike Vernal remembers the experience as an existential moment for Facebook, and a lesson in how quickly consumer technology trends can change. "When the iPhone launched, mobile looked very small. It was hard to judge mobile based on its future value, because nobody knew how big it could get. Facebook got caught flat-footed. We had to course-correct with all of our might."

The rise of mobile in 2011 struck Facebook with the Innovator's Dilemma, a term that describes the decision between building products for existing customers versus developing new innovations for a future customer base. In 2011, Facebook's existing desktop customers were future mobile users, so the answer was obvious: no more hedging on HTML5.

"I think the first mistake people make in the Innovator's Dilemma is failing to pay attention to things that are small," concludes Mike Vernal. "I think you really have to burn the boats and move over to the other thing with all of your might."

# 2

# PORTFOLIO MANAGEMENT

*"Facebook has been an incredibly innovative company because its engineering values system enables it to embrace risk."*

—JOCELYN GOLDFEIN

The four critical years of Facebook's transition from desktop to mobile occurred between 2010 and 2014.

Over these four years, Facebook explored several different business models as it searched for a new cash cow. Facebook's revenue in 2010 came primarily from desktop advertising. In order to complete its pivot to mobile, Facebook would need to develop a new business model suited to a world where mobile usage dominated.

By the end of 2012, Facebook was starting to run mobile

ads. At $73 million in annual revenue, the results of mobile advertising were promising but not tremendous. Facebook was making almost the same amount of money from payments flowing through its desktop gaming platform. And both of these revenue sources were dwarfed by desktop advertising, the dominant source of Facebook's $5 billion revenue in 2012.

At the same time, an hour north of Facebook campus in San Francisco, Ilya Sukhar was a few years into the development of Parse, a company he co-founded in 2011 to make cloud services for mobile developers. After studying computer science at Cornell, Ilya had worked at two different startups that had been acquired. With Parse, he was putting his startup experience to work with his own company.

Parse was a newer kind of cloud provider called "backend-as-a-service," built to simplify the complexities of Amazon Web Services and the mobile ecosystem.

"Parse made cloud services for mobile developers," says Ilya. "We wanted to make it dramatically easier to spin up an app and get all the basic functionality, particularly on the backend." When Ilya started Parse, there was a strong desire in the developer world to build mobile apps. The rest of the world was realizing what Facebook had realized: the future of consumer technology was mobile.

To build a mobile app was a frustrating process. An application backend needed cloud storage, user accounts, analytics, push notifications, and all the other functionality needed to integrate comfortably with web, iOS, and Android frontends.

Parse gave developers a smooth experience for building mobile application backends, and developers loved it. That's why Facebook decided to acquire the startup.

By 2012, Facebook had also become popular among developers. Game companies such as Zynga relied on Facebook's desktop product for distribution and payments. The model was similar to that of the iOS App Store and the Android Play Store. Developers benefitted from various distribution and growth mechanisms, and in exchange Facebook kept a percentage of all payments flowing through the system. These payments were largely for virtual goods, a surprisingly large business in 2012, making up 15 percent of Facebook revenues.

But the team responsible for this business line, the platform team, knew that this number was down from 19 percent the year before. And it would keep sliding downward as the majority of Facebook traffic swung from desktop to mobile. On the mobile platforms, Apple and Google played the role of distributor and payment facilitator. The platform team needed a new way to contribute to Facebook's success in the mobile era.

Around the company, teams wondered: would mobile advertising be enough?

Mobile is a very different experience than desktop. It is a smaller screen, so developers considered that mobile users might consume fewer ads. In 2012, mobile e-commerce had not yet developed significantly, so maybe e-commerce ads would not perform well on mobile. And there was the potential that new mobile ad blocker technology would become popular. With all of these risk factors, Facebook was unsure if mobile ads would drive the same kind of revenues that the company was seeing on desktop.

Facebook was looking for alternative business models to supplement advertising and was seriously considering a move towards cloud computing or some other kind of developer platform business.

The vision of Facebook as a developer platform made Parse an appealing acquisition target.

"Facebook had a little bit of an existential situation on their hands," says Ilya. "The whole company had not yet done the transition to mobile. That was a big question in the stock market."

Although Facebook was starting to make its technological shift to mobile, there were lots of unanswered questions about how mobile would make money for them. How would the ad units look? How should they be priced? How should Facebook's sales and marketing teams work to improve those ads?

And most importantly—did advertisers even want to buy mobile ads from Facebook?

Ilya explains the predicament that caused Facebook to eventually buy Parse. "Facebook's business model in a post-mobile world was undetermined. The core business was going to do fine for years, but it wasn't going to grow, because everything was transitioning to mobile."

While Facebook was still navigating the open questions of how to monetize its mobile user base, the platform team decided to try to explore cloud computing as a successor to its gaming payments business.

In April 2013, Facebook formally announced the acquisition of Parse. Ilya Sukhar describes the acquisition as one of several bets that Facebook was placing to answer the question of Facebook post-mobile. We were one of the experiments."

"When we sold the company to Facebook, we had somewhere between 60,000 and 80,000 active developers. Through our height at Facebook, it was a magnitude higher than that. We had all these developers, we had data centers, we had technology that was really interesting."

Facebook's vision was to use Parse as the foundation for a developer platform that could unify mobile and backend infrastructure together with Facebook's social identity platform. It was a bright future, but it was never to be realized: mobile advertising turned out to be far more lucrative than Facebook anticipated.

By the end of October 2013, just six months after Facebook announced the acquisition of Parse, Facebook mobile ad revenue had reached parity with desktop ad revenue. By the end of the year, mobile ad revenue was larger than desktop. And the platform team had run another experiment: creating an ad unit that allowed developers to pay for installs of their mobile apps. It was a huge success within months. Across the company, the anxiety around the viability of mobile advertising melted away.

Online advertising businesses are notoriously hard to build, but when they are successful they generate more cash than almost any other Internet business model, including cloud infrastructure. Once it was clear that mobile advertising would be a powerful business for Facebook, the company centralized all of its spare resources on building the cash cow.

With the success of mobile ads, Parse fell by the wayside.

Ilya sighs. At the time, he felt conflicted: his acquirer's stock would now be worth much more, but his company had to be subsumed in the process. "No matter how well Parse did, no matter how much developer love we had, how many apps we had, how many users of those apps we had, how much revenue we were making—at the end of the day, it's really hard to compete with a well-oiled ad business. Ad businesses are very efficient. Very, very efficient."

Parse found itself under the control of an owner that now had no reason to invest in a cloud infrastructure platform. Facebook had crossed the chasm into the post-mobile world. "The company had made the transition. Stock was up a ton, printing money, newsfeed working great, newsfeed ads working great, app install ads working great for the platform team."

As engineering headcount was increasingly allocated to teams working on mobile and advertising infrastructure, Parse's resources dwindled.

Ilya is sanguine about the experience. "An engineer put toward ad targeting, put toward the core business at that time was just a way better investment for Facebook. I can't really argue with that. I think the most fundamental explanation is that Facebook didn't really need Parse. Fundamentally, the company moved on. It's hard to say exactly when, but I think the Parse acquisition somewhat became irrelevant over the time we were there."

Ilya was not happy about the situation. His own business had become a casualty of the acquirer's success.

"It hurt a lot. At the time it was just brutally painful. If you had lopped us off, just cut us off and made us an independent company again, I think we would be a very strong startup."

Ilya expresses respect for Facebook. Mobile ads are a huge cash cow, with much higher expected value than cloud services divisions. Facebook had shifted its mentality from a hedging strategy to one of complete focus on mobile advertising. Parse was no longer a hedge—it had become a distraction.

Ilya gives his high-level conclusions of what makes Facebook a successful company. "Facebook made a decision to try things. If they didn't take off quickly, those things were abandoned."

"When I was at Facebook, the company's core strength seemed to be Mark Zuckerberg's management orientation. Every six months he had a few priorities. He oriented the company around those priorities. Teams got shuffled. Sometimes, messes were left behind. But we were always super focused on the strategic priorities. We were intellectually honest about where the leverage was in the system. I think there are a lot of advantages to that. It worked. It's hard to argue with."

# 3

# THREATS

*"Here is a key insight for any startup: You may think yourself a puny midget among giants when you stride out into a marketplace, and suddenly confront such a giant via direct competition. But the reality is that larger companies often have much more to fear from you than you from them. For starters, their will to fight is less than yours. Their employees are mercenaries who don't deeply care, and suffer from the diffuse responsibility and weak emotional investment of a larger organization. What's an existential struggle to you is merely one more set of tasks to a tuned-out engineer bored of his own product."*

—ANTONIO GARCIA MARTINEZ, *CHAOS MONKEYS: OBSCENE FORTUNE AND RANDOM FAILURE IN SILICON VALLEY*

Facebook's pivot to mobile was a response to an industry-wide shift in consumer preferences.

When consumers started using mobile devices, the smartphone was not directly competing with Facebook. Facebook was not so much concerned about a competitor as it was worried that users would simply stop using their product. The company's worries about mobile throughout 2011 were mostly introspective rather than external.

In June 2011, Facebook encountered a directly offensive threat: Google+.

Google+ was a social network that Google built with a design very similar to Facebook's. It had a newsfeed, a chat system, and groups. Back in 2011, many people throughout the world had not yet adopted social networking. A user picking their first social network might easily pick Google+.

As Google+ launched, every other Google product was slowly integrated with its social features.

Google Search results displayed a "+1" button that allowed you to socially endorse them to your friends. Gmail encouraged you to follow your family members after you sent them an email. YouTube, and Chrome, and Hangouts, and every other Google product made it clear that Google was making a strong push to become a social networking company.

Google was launching a full assault on Facebook's walled garden of social network content. The threat of Google+

was an affront to the creative sensibilities of Facebook employees. They felt they were being attacked directly, which filled them with enthusiasm.

During my interviews with Facebook engineers, I repeatedly asked the question: what makes Google and Facebook engineering different from one another? One answer is the DNA of the founders. Facebook was hacked together by an undergrad building a PHP application. Google was architected by a pair of PhD students in computer science.

In 2012, there was a corporate Facebook bus stop in San Francisco's Mission District, directly across the street from a corporate Google bus stop. Facebook engineers would crowd into the bus like an unruly mob of schoolchildren. Google engineers would line up outside of their bus in an orderly queue. This image of the patient line of Googlers across the street from the disorganized Facebook employees encapsulates the personalities of the respective companies.

From its early days, Google has had more of an air of "computer science," an academic bent that emphasizes proofs, correctness, and seriousness. Facebook engineers are self-deprecating hackers who just want to build cool stuff. Facebook engineers are comfortable with the fact that sometimes things break, and sometimes mistakes are made.

When Facebook employees talk about the difficulties of the mobile pivot, there is a slight sense of humor. With the benefit of hindsight, it's easy for them to see that trying to build performant mobile apps with HTML5 was a mistake. It was simply an error in judgment. With today's knowledge, they laugh it off.

But when it comes to Google+, Facebook engineers become deadly serious. Google+ was a blatant clone that Google was pushing out through its existing distribution channels. Facebook engineers were disgusted. One of those engineers was Keith Adams.

Keith Adams is an infrastructure engineer with a quiet, academic demeanor. After joining Facebook in 2009, Keith eventually became a legend as the creator of HHVM, a system for running PHP code more effectively. Understated, peaceful, and humble, he is the kind of engineer of whom you would never feel scared. But when reminded of Google+, even a pacifist like Keith narrows his eyes and becomes energized with a competitive spirit.

Keith describes the rivalrous history that led to the creation of Google+. "There was a drum beat building inside of Google to destroy Facebook. It wasn't just an effort to get into social networking. They were focused on us. Google wanted to destroy us."

In the world of software warfare, there are not many rules of engagement. The corporate battle between Google and Facebook had gotten dirty. Google was aggressively scraping the Facebook social graph, mapping out how Facebook worked and what made it successful. Around this time, Google gave its engineers a 10 percent raise across the board. Facebook followed suit a few weeks later.

By early 2011, Facebook engineers heard that Google was planning to launch Google+. Suspense began building within Facebook, as the employees awaited the fateful launch.

"I remember it feeling really scary," says Keith. "Google was enormously larger, enormously more resourced, and willing to do anything to defeat us, including building a straight up Facebook clone. That's what was alarming. This was a Facebook clone, except it was built by Google engineers. Google engineers are intimidating. They are ten feet tall. They eat razor blades for breakfast. How could we compete?"

Was this how the Facebook story would end? Would Facebook users rapidly migrate over into Google+? Would Facebook dissolve into the past, absorbed like a feature in the vast, omnipotent Google empire?

The Google+ launch is documented in the acclaimed book *Chaos Monkeys* by Antonio Garcia Martinez. Antonio is the gonzo journalist of Silicon Valley, a mercurial entrepreneur with a cynic's taste for cheap alcohol and Tenderloin bar hopping. He is a tortured artist, a deceptive businessman, and an unreliable narrator. Nonetheless, Antonio is one of the most honest writers to document the human realities of the booming tech industry.

Antonio worked at Facebook as a product manager and had been with the company for a few months when Google+ launched. He remembers the day vividly.

"Google+ was prettier than Facebook," says Antonio. "It integrated tightly with all of the Google services: email, search, everything. Google had an obvious advantage, and Facebook had never faced any serious competitors, so this was a new kind of existential threat. It was intimidating."

Antonio recalls how the dumpy industrial building which served as Facebook campus suddenly felt like a military barracks under siege. "Out of the blue, we get an email from Zuckerberg saying: 'Everybody meet outside the main conference room.' It was a vague email, so we didn't know exactly what it was about. We all crowded into the middle of the engineering bullpen in the main building. And Zuckerberg comes out and gives a rousing speech about Google+."

Antonio notes the influence that Roman warrior rhetoric had on Zuckerberg's style of speaking. "Zuckerberg was

always a fan of Pliny the Elder and other famous historical speakers. And you could hear it in his voice, as he
announced that there would be weekend meal service, and
that everyone would need to be working 24/7 to fend off
this threat."

Even Antonio felt inspired by Zuckerberg's speech, and
he happily woke up on Sunday morning and drove to the
Facebook offices. He arrived to a packed parking lot, and
struggled to find a space for his car. He wondered if Google's parking lot was as full as Facebook's.

He hopped back on the 101 and shot south, getting off at
Shoreline Drive to go see Google Campus, and found the
parking lot completely empty. Nobody was showing up on
Sunday to work on Google+. "It was clear then that Google
was not playing to win," says Antonio.

As Google rested on its laurels, Facebook went into full-on
wartime mode. Battle posters throughout the Facebook
campus kept employees on high alert, a constant reminder
that everything they had worked for could be devastated
by Google. These posters were so popular that they would
be stolen on a weekly basis, and Facebook would have to
print new ones.

Antonio describes the Facebook campus taking on a charac-
teristic of Rome prior to its war with Carthage. A legendary

Latin phrase uttered by a Roman politician is, "Carthago delanda est:" Carthage must be destroyed. Zuckerberg had embodied the spirit of the politicians who roused Rome to destroy Carthage. Antonio has a wry smile on his face. "Google delanda est, as it were."

Engineers who were at Facebook during the early days of Google+ remember the fervent enthusiasm. The company was ready to defend its territory, and everyone had bought into the mission. Facebook's execution on products became as honed as a dagger, as the company improved its mobile platform and figured out its business model.

Users never fell in love with Google+. Despite the Google product experience becoming saturated with features that directed the user towards Google+, it never seemed to have the satisfying stickiness of the Facebook product.

When I ask Mike Vernal why Google+ failed, he pauses and thinks deeply, thinking back to his time as a director of engineering at Facebook. "It's hard to be excellent at two different types of products with the same company culture. It would have been hard for Google to be excellent at social while also being excellent at search."

After Google+ failed to gain traction, the product was eventually discontinued. Google spent years deprecating

Google+, removing all of the integrations that had been bolted onto other Google products.

In retrospect, everyone realizes just how damaging Google+ was to the overall Google product experience. Before Google+, Google offered a set of clean utilities: search, email, videos, and maps. Google's product suite fades into the background of your life as you become completely reliant on its services.

With Google+, the Google product experience started to feel like a petulant copycat. Consumers could feel the shamelessness of Google+. And perhaps the engineers at Google could feel it too. If Google engineers truly felt that they needed to obliterate Facebook, there would have been far more cars in the Google parking lot that Sunday.

The story of Google+ illustrates the tension that technology companies feel when it comes to the word "competition."

It is common sense in modern business strategy that companies should be customer-focused rather than competitor-focused. When Google tried to compete directly with Facebook, Google not only failed to win, but it made its product actively worse.

On the other hand, Facebook accepted the direct challenge and went to war with Google. With Google as a competitor, Facebook employees worked harder than ever before, convinced that they were in a zero-sum battle for social network supremacy. Zero-sum competitions can motivate an employee base for some period of time, but what happens when you destroy the enemy? Can a company with a zero-sum focus stay motivated after a bout of competition?

Apparently, this was not a problem for Facebook, because Facebook's culture is fundamentally positive-sum. For Facebook, crushing Google+ was merely a speed bump on the road to building more cool stuff. One thing I admire about Facebook engineers is that they all seem to live by the dictum expressed by Mark Zuckerberg in 2012: "We don't build services to make money. We make money to build services."

Although Facebook was temporarily fixated on beating Google, the company never lost sight of its main purpose: building new products, designing new experiences, and growing user engagement.

# EXPERIMENT
# AND ITERATE

*"Software is not a destination. The process never ends. We are never going to reach some utopian state where everything is perfectly satisfying."*

—TOM OCCHINO, FACEBOOK ENGINEERING DIRECTOR

Facebook's mobile ad business is a cash cow.

Broadly defined, a cash cow is an income stream that generates a large amount of money relative to the funds required to run that line of business. Google's biggest cash cow is the "AdWords" search ads business. Amazon's biggest cash cow is Amazon Web Services.

Many companies are built without a large cash cow, and a business does not necessarily need one to gain traction.

When a software company does not have a cash cow, its main priority is to figure out how to develop one. From 2011 to 2012, Facebook was looking for a cash cow business model that would grow with the rise of mobile.

Once the mobile ads business started to work in late 2012, Facebook could safely expect revenues to grow with the expansion of mobile. Such a durable revenue stream put Facebook in a position where its large cash flows could be used to fund experimentation with products such as virtual reality, low-flying Internet drones, and neural interfaces. Even these costly explorations are a rounding error compared to the volume of cash generated from mobile advertising.

But Facebook has been experimenting with new products since the beginning of its existence. A quick search for "Facebook failed products" reveals products such as 2011's "Facebook Deals," which was a Groupon competitor, and "Facebook Gifts," a service for buying physical gifts for your friends that was cancelled in 2013.

Facebook's habit of experimentation helped it find a cash cow. Now that the company has one, its culture of exploration ensures that new product ideas continually bubble up from within the company.

As novel products emerge through a process of continuous experimentation, the products that show promise are iterated on and improved. The products that don't gain traction are abandoned.

After a project finds some minimal amount of success, Facebook can choose to invest more resources into it. This allows the company to iterate on a project, gradually moving it towards a place that can be seen by users.

During the iteration process, a project matures. Bugs are ironed out. Small hypotheses are tested. It usually takes a long period of iteration for a "project" to mature into a "product."

At Facebook, new products are often developed in a bottom-up fashion. An individual engineer might see an opportunity and devote some time to trying it out with a prototype. The prototype is often developed because an engineer decides to work nights and weekends to build something adjunct to their day-to-day work. In other cases, an engineer might receive permission from their manager to spend a few weeks tinkering on a prototype.

Facebook's creative process is also systematized through hackathons. A hackathon is an event where employees are free to work on whatever they please. Many of Facebook's features and products started as hackathon projects.

Hackathons can yield prototype products that eventually

change an organization. But a prototype version of a product is rarely good enough to confirm whether customers will actually want it. A prototype is useful for showing the experimental version of what a product will end up looking like.

Most projects die during the prototype stage.

The engineer who develops the prototype often loses interest in the project after seeing how hard it is to build. Or perhaps the prototype version is so much worse than what the engineer imagined that the engineer becomes confused, disgusted, or dispirited.

The prototyping phase is a gauge of how serious the engineer is going to be about bringing something into existence. It is also an important point of contact between the creativity of an engineer and the innovation culture of the company.

To get from prototype to finished product requires iteration. To run useful experiments, a company must also invest in cycles of iteration, bringing a product fully to market and putting it in contact with users.

Pete Hunt is a Facebook engineer who joined the company in 2011. Pete is six-foot-four with a towering frame and a curly mop of hair. His default expression is a lighthearted, goofy smile, but Pete becomes a serious, imposing figure once he starts to discuss matters of software. Today, Pete's reputation among engineers precedes him. Large crowds gather at his conference talks, and his Internet comments about JavaScript frameworks are widely quoted.

But back in 2011, Pete was just a new engineer looking to prove himself.

When he joined Facebook, Pete started working on Facebook Video. "Video was a hackathon project from two or three years before I joined and nobody was maintaining it. It wasn't a source of revenue for the company."

At some point in Facebook history, a small team at a Facebook hackathon had put together a system to upload and play videos on Facebook. After the hackathon, there was a time period in which Facebook Video was a functional product but not a high enough priority for the company to assign engineering resources to it.

Facebook Video existed in a nebulous space between prototype and finished product. It was accessible to users but not widely seen or promoted through newsfeed.

Although Facebook Video was not an exciting product when Pete began working on it, he saw the obvious potential for video on Facebook. "Facebook was always trying to ship the minimum viable product, and that was where Facebook Video was at when I started working on it."

Shortly after Pete started working on Video, the product rapidly improved. With iteration, Facebook Video became more closely integrated with the rest of the Facebook product, which caused more users to see and use it. Today, Facebook users watch millions of videos on Facebook every day. Facebook Video generates advertising revenue for the company and has a significant amount of resources allocated to it.

Pete describes iteration as broadly important to Facebook's success.

"Facebook is a large-scale consumer application that is written on a stack that is fast and easy to deploy. Faster deployment means faster iterations. When you are building a consumer product, there are lots of competitors. You need to be able to develop products fast to respond to competition and keep up. So you want to create an engineering organization and a set of values in a culture that biases towards rapid iteration and moving quickly."

To move from prototype project to finished product, Pete emphasizes the need to put a product in front of users as quickly as possible. "If you're not sure whether you should ship or not, you should ship, get the data. Ship it to a small test group. Get some data, roll it back if it sucks. The whole company was organized around that."

Even in cases of complete product failure, Facebook will often learn from the experiment in a way that provides significant value.

In 2011, just as Facebook was making its pivot into mobile, Instagram was starting to gain traction. Facebook assumed that it could build a product to compete with Instagram, and created Facebook Camera, a standalone camera-first mobile app. Despite focused iteration, Facebook Camera failed to gain traction. This was an indication that Facebook could not simply replicate Instagram's success in-house.

After pushing Facebook Camera through the prototyping phase and bringing it into contact with the market, Facebook had a firsthand understanding of the social photos market. With this insight, the company felt comfortable in its assessment that Instagram was underpriced, even at $1 billion. With thirteen employees, Instagram could have seemed dramatically overpriced if not for Facebook's firsthand experience trying to compete against it.

Today, Facebook is in a luxurious position when it comes to building new products.

Not only does Facebook have a highly profitable cash cow

in its advertising business, but Facebook has access to a treasure trove of interesting data, and engineers at Facebook can study the data and build products using a wide selection of cutting-edge tools. With all of these resources, it's easy for Facebook to experiment.

Can the average company learn anything about experimentation from Facebook? Most companies don't have billions of dollars rolling in from ad revenue. Most companies feel too constrained by the day-to-day operations of their business to run a hackathon.

A culture of experimentation allows a business without a cash cow to find a strong source of revenue. Experimentation also enables a business that already has a cash cow to find additional sources of revenue. But experimentation is not just about improving the balance sheet—it is critical to the psychological health of a company.

A strong engineering organization must have an outlet for engineers to let out creative steam.

The best engineers are often tortured by a constant stream of good ideas in their head. A good engineer who does software maintenance every day starts to feel their dreams evaporate and can lose their motivation. Such an engineer will often leave their company and find a place that gives them freedom to invent.

If an organization does not encourage engineers to experiment routinely, the engineering culture will select engineers who lack the ability or motivation to experiment. The company will erode into maintenance mode and die a slow death.

But even for companies that want to experiment, it is difficult to judge how many experiments to run and how large those experiments should be. A new employee usually gets hired to work on some preexisting challenge within the company. A salesperson gets hired to sell existing products. An engineer gets hired to improve those existing products. Should an employee's time ever be devoted to prototyping new products?

There is no simple method for promoting a culture of experimentation, because experimentation must be balanced against the day-to-day operations of the business. To understand how Facebook fits experimentation into its overall product strategy, we need to take a holistic view of the company's culture.

# PART 2

# CULTURE

# 5

# SOMETHING HAPPENS

*"Nobody is sure anymore who really runs the company (not even the people who are credited with running it), but the company does run."*

—JOSEPH HELLER, *SOMETHING HAPPENED*

Culture is very hard to scale.

Since the dot com boom, popular books have told the stories of successful cultural scalability: Netflix, Apple, Google, and Amazon. These companies have all been able to grow from a startup to a large company without sacrificing their culture of innovation.

There are also tales of dramatic company disaster, such as Theranos and Enron. These companies started out aspiring to innovation, only to be brought down by toxic company culture.

These stories of cultural extremes are exciting. But none of them explore the most common negative attributes that can develop in big company culture: boredom, office politics, and a general sense of stagnation.

What is it really like to be an average employee inside of a large company? One answer lies in a work of fiction: *Something Happened* by Joseph Heller.

In 1961, Joseph Heller captured the existential dread that employees at large corporations often feel. In *Something Happened*, middling employee Bob Slocum works for a large American business and finds his life slowly losing meaning. Bob is the narrator of the book, and the reader gets a constant window into his state of mind.

The title of the book refers to the fact that something happens to an employee at a large corporation: the employee wakes up one day to find their personal dreams dissolved. This quote from Bob Slocum summarizes his state of constant, blasé hopelessness: "Something did happen to me somewhere that robbed me of confidence and courage and left me with a fear of discovery and change and a positive dread of everything unknown that may occur."

At work, Bob spends more time deciphering the office gossip and petty internal feuds than he does building any kind of value for the company. He decides that office politics are the best means of advancing within the company. And yet his focus on office politics distracts him from doing anything of actual substance—a fact which scares him to death because it may get him fired. Bob anxiously discusses his internal state: "I have a feeling that someone nearby is soon going to find out something about me that will mean the end, although I can't imagine what that something is."

In Bob Slocum's world, employees are able to advance despite doing nothing of substance to benefit the company. Employees think only in political terms, about what will allow them to stay at the company rather than what will allow the company to grow.

Sadly, most employees throughout the world would identify more with the dreary cubicles portrayed in *Something Happened* than the caffeinated excitement of the San Francisco startup life. And yet these two extremes of paranoid misery and passionate creativity are opposite evolutionary states of the same organism: the modern corporation.

A startup begins with a joyous, tight-knit team. The team innovates, makes a product, closes deals, and grows to employ thousands of people. But somewhere along the way, something happens. The startup becomes a "big company." Employees start to dread coming into work.

A naive reader of Joseph Heller's book *Something Happened* might think the book is satire. But once you have sat in the cubicles, listening to the office gossip, feeling the tedium of software maintenance work, you will know the truth: the corporate workplace of 2020 is in some ways the same as it was sixty years ago.

Is this state of office stagnation unavoidable? Or can we reach a balance? Can companies get big without losing the fun camaraderie they had when they were small?

Fortunately, we have reason to be optimistic. There are a handful of large companies that have managed to systematize and scale the creative spirit that is so treasured by early employees of a startup. Facebook is one of these companies.

Facebook's culture enables creative individuals to coexist with a large corporate workforce with clear focus and direction. Throughout my interviews with Facebook employees, a few themes emerged.

Facebook places a strong focus on individuals. Company management tries to ensure that individuals feel creatively fulfilled. Facebook employees have a strong sense of social cohesion, both across the company and within individual teams. This is possible because employees across the organization truly believe they are doing something important. Facebook's product direction is set from the top down, but individual employees have the freedom and the motivation for bottom-up innovation.

Facebook also has a set of unique cultural norms, including "code wins arguments." These norms are quickly ingrained in new employees during an onboarding program known as boot camp.

Surveying the Facebook culture, it seems remarkably deliberate. Facebook has been able to scale its culture through specific decisions, not by accident.

# 6

# INDIVIDUALS

*"Yes, it's Facebook. The work is fun. But there's stuff that you don't want to do, and it needs to get done."*

—NICK SCHROCK, FORMER FACEBOOK ENGINEER

Every employee wants to feel creatively fulfilled in their job, and every company has a large amount of unfulfilling work that needs to get done. How can a company satisfy the needs of the individual employee while also making progress on company objectives?

Tom Occhino has worked at Facebook for eleven years. Today, he is the engineering director of the React group, an open source infrastructure division of Facebook that includes React Core, React Native, and other related projects. Tom is friendly and encouraging, with the winning smile of your favorite high school guidance counselor, and he has earned the respect of the React group through a combination of technical knowledge and empathy.

"I optimize for engineers doing work that they love." Tom believes that engineers should be spending 75 percent of their time at work on things that they are passionate about, because engineers do their best work when they are creatively satisfied.

From Tom's perspective, management cannot blindly assign work based on what needs to be done. Individual preferences need to be accounted for. People do their best work when they don't feel like they're just another cog in the machine.

Tom Occhino's team is staffed with some of the best engineers in the world. But even so, it's never the case that everybody is perfectly happy with everything that they're working on and the team is having the maximum possible impact on Facebook.

There are exciting greenfield projects to build, but there are also boring bugs. And unfortunately, someone is going to have to fix those bugs. As Tom says, "Engineering work is a stable matching problem and it's in constant evolution."

If an engineer cannot find any work they enjoy within their current team, there is a well-defined process for moving to another. "We literally call it engineering mobility," says Tom. "After an engineer has been on the same team for a year, we encourage them to take what we call a hack-a-month and try out the experience of being on a different team. If you don't like that team, you can go back to your old team, or you can try something else."

Tom is a popular manager, so much of his team will stick within the React group. Even within that single team, there are so many different projects at all areas of the stack that many engineers never get bored.

Over time, projects begin and end. Engineers get moved from project to project, from subteam to subteam. If Tom keeps these people satisfied, a sense of mutual respect develops between him and each of his direct reports.

When he gives employees the kind of work they enjoy, Tom earns the trust of his fellow engineers. And when he earns their trust, he knows that these engineers will be willing to pick up unpleasant tasks when necessary. "If I come to them with an engineering crisis, they will support me. They will do the work that needs to get done, even if it's not their number one choice."

I have spoken to multiple engineers who have worked for Tom, and it's clear he is an amazing manager. The React team sounds like a utopia of engineering satisfaction.

Could it be possible for a manager with the charisma of Tom Occhino to keep his team happy with their assigned tasks 75 percent of the time?

As I interviewed Facebook engineers, I imagined myself as an employee at Facebook. How would I respond to the environment of the company? Would I have enough individual expression through my engineering work to feel creatively satisfied?

Tom Occhino still works at Facebook, so it is possible he was not telling me the full story about how happy the engineers are with their work. I needed to know more about how corporate goals clash with the requirements of individuality, and I knew that I could trust Pete Hunt to give me an answer less colored by allegiance to Facebook.

After leaving Facebook, Pete started an anti-spam company that was eventually acquired by Twitter. Pete is an entrepreneur and a musician, and his Facebook photo features his towering frame with a guitar on stage, his mop of curls sitting over a goofy, smiling face. Pete is an artist at heart, and he knows how unpleasant it can be to be an artistic engineer trapped in a cubicle doing software maintenance.

When I ask Pete about how realistic it is for an engineer to be happy with their assigned tasks 75 percent of the time, his expression turns from a goofy smile to a gravely honest frown. "If I'm managing an engineer, I expect them to be mature," says Pete. "And with some projects, it's not going to be the most interesting thing in the world, but we need you to work on it for a while, and we need you to have some patience and not be a diva about it."

Pete explains that at Facebook, the product surface area is huge, and there are thousands of problems to explore. Engineers are given the freedom to find something that interests them. An engineer with a strong track record can even decide to run their own experiment.

But in the end, everybody needs to justify their presence at the company in terms of real business impact.

Low performers are fired from Facebook pretty easily. Facebook tries to give these engineers the time they need to find an engaging project within the company, but it simply doesn't always work out.

Engineering satisfaction is in the eye of the beholder. Some individuals are happy doing software maintenance, and some individuals will never be happy even if they are working on the product of their dreams.

# BOOTCAMP

*"Bootcamp allowed Facebook to maintain its cultural identity as it went from tens, to hundreds, to thousands, to tens of thousands of people."*

—PEDRAM KEYANI, FORMER FACEBOOK
ENGINEERING DIRECTOR

When an engineer starts working at Facebook, the first few weeks of employee onboarding take place at Facebook bootcamp, a program in which the engineer is introduced to the engineering standards and best practices of Facebook.

A bootcamp engineer needs to fix real Facebook issues and ship real code to production, and there is pressure on them to get moving quickly. But the term "bootcamp" makes it sound much more brutal than it is. Bootcamp is a safe environment in which engineers become familiar with the nuances of Facebook's tooling and infrastructure. A boot-camp engineer is encouraged to ask questions.

Bootcamp also gives new engineers a period of time to ramp up with the fast pace of the company while training in a supportive environment, with senior engineers available to help the onboarding process go as smoothly as possible.

Bootcamp is a sharp departure from how engineering works at most large software organizations.

When a software engineer joins a typical large organization, months pass before any of the engineer's code is shipped out to real users. From the engineer's earliest days at the organization, they receive an implicit signal that the release process is slow and that they need to earn trust before they can push code to production.

At Facebook, engineers are expected to ship code within their first few days of bootcamp. This sets expectations for the speed at which an engineer will make meaningful contributions to Facebook's codebase.

In order for an engineer to be self-reliant and make an impact, they need to feel confident in their ability to push through the entire process of writing code, getting it peer reviewed, and releasing it to users.

For a new engineer, the process of pushing code to the production environment can be scary. If you make a mistake, you could theoretically take down the entire Facebook platform.

During Facebook bootcamp, the engineer learns the code review and release process in a safe environment. Bootcamp can significantly decrease the time-to-productivity for a new engineer. This speedy onboarding process lasts for six weeks and allows engineers to start adding value to the company much sooner than might otherwise be the case.

In today's software industry, many employees only stay at a job for eighteen months or less. Onboarding to a typical company often takes three months, and only after that period can the employee start to add significant value. When an engineer spends three months learning the internal engineering stack, the organization misses out on one-fifth of the value they could otherwise contribute.

By standardizing the onboarding process, Facebook lowers the cost of onboarding by making it a smaller overall percentage of an engineer's time at the company.

When a software engineer joins a new company, there is a tendency to take whatever made them successful at the previous company and apply it in their new work. This causes problems. Every software company has its own style. Just because you built software at Google does not mean you know how to build software at Facebook.

Everyone must go through bootcamp, whether you just graduated from college or you are an industry veteran with twenty years of experience. Bootcamp is a great equalizer in this way. A computer scientist with a PhD might join Facebook and spend a week fixing CSS bugs. An author of a textbook on artificial intelligence might need to struggle through setting up a MySQL database.

Bootcamp sends the message that no matter who you are, you do the work that the organization needs. But there is also another purpose of bootcamp: to help individual engineers find work within Facebook that they enjoy.

In bootcamp, the new engineer gets exposed to multiple different teams, including product teams and internal tools teams. Thus, the engineer is able to find a team that is a good fit for their work style and desired career goals. In this way, Facebook optimizes for the individual satisfaction of new employees.

Bootcamp is not designed to be difficult. Unlike a bootcamp for the army, Facebook bootcamp does not try to filter out engineers. The filtering process occurs before the engineer is hired.

Getting a job at Facebook is very difficult. In order to get hired, a prospective candidate needs to write code on a whiteboard, answer questions about software architecture, and display an understanding of Facebook culture. Most people who apply to Facebook do not receive an interview. Most people who receive an interview do not get hired.

Once an engineer has made it through this difficult process, they have earned an alliance with Facebook: they are hired. And once an engineer is hired, Facebook starts to do everything possible to make sure that the new hire is successful. That includes helping the engineer find a position within the company that they will truly enjoy.

Bootcamp allows new employees to sample different teams before the employee commits to joining a team. This is notably different from the traditional hiring process. At most companies, you are applying to a specific job on a specific team. At Facebook, you get hired as a general purpose Facebook engineer. Then, you go through bootcamp and find a job you will enjoy.

When an engineer is searching for a job, it is not easy to predict in advance whether a given team will be a good fit. You need to work on a team for a while in order to understand the codebase, the internal team culture, and the demands. There is simply no substitute for actually doing this work.

Some teams have intense on-call schedules, and their engineers often get phone calls in the middle of the night. Some teams have a terribly boring set of problems to solve, so their engineers are able to coast, only really working fifteen hours a week. Which team is a good fit for you?

With bootcamp, Facebook avoids a toxic problem that plagues many software companies: the misleading job description.

A talented engineer is always getting bombarded with recruiter emails. These emails often describe a job opportunity in exciting yet unrealistic terms. For example, a shifty recruiter might talk about a job that is "reinventing the future of communications" when the job actually entails fixing old spaghetti code for sending people spam text messages.

At these tech companies, there is an incentive misalignment between the recruiters and the engineers they are recruiting. Recruiters might be rewarded simply for an engineer getting hired—not for whether the engineer is happy once they find out what their job actually entails.

Typical recruitment processes at big companies can mislead employees into taking on boring work that they come to despise.

After an engineer gets recruited to a boring job, employment norms keep them at the company for fifteen months. Internal transfers are difficult to get approved before twelve months, so the engineer is stuck. The end result of this is that the boring work gets accomplished, but the employee becomes resentful of the company.

If you are a young engineer, you are more likely to fall victim to a misleading job description. When a young engineer sees a job posting that advertises "reinventing the future of communications," they don't know any better. Young engineers are drawn to companies with a strong brand name, lured into working on mind-numbing legacy code, and accustomed to the idea that software engineering is drudgery.

In the United States, H1-B immigrants are exploited even more severely by misleading job descriptions.

The H1-B is a work visa that allows international employees to work in fields such as engineering. Many of the best software engineers in the world come to the United States with multiple job offers from different tech companies. Once an H1-B engineer commits to working at a particular company, it is very hard for them to switch to another. And as soon as an H1-B immigrant becomes unemployed, they must leave the country. So an H1-B engineer must choose their job carefully.

An H1-B immigrant who is considering jobs at several large tech companies does not know which of the job descriptions are real and which ones are misleading. In practice, this leads to brilliant H1-B knowledge workers assigned to some of the most brutally boring engineering work available in the United States.

At Facebook, the bootcamp process has alleviated this. New hires are not assigned to a role until they have shown themselves to be a good fit with a specific team.

When engineers have the freedom to choose what they work on, it keeps them from feeling marginalized or trapped in a job they do not enjoy.

The other side of bootcamp is a system called "headcount." Every team within Facebook is allocated a headcount number, which defines how many engineers the team is allowed to bring on. If a team is mission critical, that team might get a large headcount number. If the team is less important, their headcount might be just two or three at a given time.

During bootcamp, the new engineers trial their relationships with different teams that have available headcount. If a team has a headcount allocation of two, then two engineers might end up joining that team after bootcamp.

In order to build a strong team, team managers need to

attract talent. A manager gets a headcount allocation for their team, but that does not guarantee that the team will be able to hire new engineers. A manager must sell their project to prospective team members. If you can't create a compelling reason for an engineer to join your team, you won't be able to hire anyone out of bootcamp.

At Facebook, nobody forces an engineer to join a team. The managers who can't sell their projects end up with bad teams and have trouble succeeding. This causes bad managers to get weeded out quickly.

Together, bootcamp and headcount systematically reward the best projects and the best managers.

For a highly regarded manager such as Tom Occhino, this process means that his open headcount is quickly noticed by bootcamp graduates. There is a steady stream of engineers from bootcamp who want to join Tom's team, which makes the React group resilient to turnover. If an engineer wants to leave Tom's team, he knows there will soon be an influx of new bootcamp graduates eager to work on React.

Bootcamp and headcount are only possible because Facebook is growing so quickly. At an average company, there might not be the steady influx of engineers, nor the plethora of interesting projects that make the two programs function in tandem.

Still, any company leader can internalize some of the concepts that Facebook has put into practice through bootcamp, namely the systematic onboarding of new employees at the level of both technology and culture.

If a company does not take deliberate steps to maintain its software culture, that culture will dissolve.

It might not be possible for most other companies to develop something so rigorous and programmatic as bootcamp. But it is at least worth the effort to think about how to codify culture and how to bring new employees up to speed as quickly as possible.

# 8

# SOCIAL COHESION

*"When you accept a job offer with Facebook, you're not accept-ing a job offer with the search team, or the Messenger team, you're accepting a job offer with Facebook."*

—JOCELYN GOLDFEIN, FORMER FACEBOOK
ENGINEERING DIRECTOR

Facebook encourages individuality at the employee level but a sense of cohesion across the company.

Cohesion does not mean that Facebook is a hive mind of people all thinking identically. Employees are extremely individualistic. Differences in opinion are encouraged. Cohesion is about a shared mission, common values within the organization, and a basic willingness to work together productively.

The hiring bar for Facebook is extremely high for technical

talent, but employees must also display a particular kind of personality. The organization values friendliness, openness, and clarity of communication.

One of Facebook's keepers of cultural history is Arturo Bejar.

Arturo Bejar is a widely celebrated former engineering director at Facebook. Empathetic, goateed, and deeply reflective, Arturo speaks with a placid tone of voice, a calmness that comes from fifteen years of managing engineers who could be both brilliant and extremely difficult to work with.

In the world of software, the most creative people are often opinionated and mercurial.

Software engineers spend lots of time in their own heads, and sometimes their trains of thought run wild. Like cloistered artists, these engineers can create abstractions of true beauty but can also have erratic, ill-conceived ideas. Arturo has learned to counterbalance the extreme personalities he manages by embodying a warm, even-keeled impartiality.

Arturo spent his early career at Yahoo, working on security engineering. At Facebook, he worked on internal tools that helped deal with suicide prevention, online bullying, and other difficult parts of online life. Facebook users open their hearts and minds across the social network, and Arturo's projects helped keep users safe.

During his six years at the company, he also started the Product Infrastructure team, which created React and GraphQL, two of the most influential open source technologies to come out of Facebook.

Despite his deeply technical background, my conversation with Arturo had almost nothing to do with software. Arturo is fascinated by the human characteristics of what makes a company successful.

This focus on human dynamics is shared among other senior engineering leaders with whom I have spoken.

There seems to be a level of enlightenment reached by the most sophisticated engineering managers, at which point the technical challenges fade into the background, and the primary concern becomes how to lead engineers towards success.

"Facebook has a very healthy social fabric," says Arturo. "Everybody that Facebook hires is socially intelligent. You can see it at lunchtime, in how people eat together. You can see it in the way teams relate to each other. And it is very important, because it's hard to build a social product if you are not a social person."

Arturo emphasizes that Facebook's culture is deliberate. "I think it's important to be cautious and clear about the culture you want to create. You have to be decisive, because you cannot be all things to all people."

By the time an engineer leaves bootcamp, they have already picked up on the cultural norms and engineering practices of the company. Facebook's stringent hiring and onboarding process ensures a kind of social quality control, says Arturo. "Getting hired at Facebook is hard. If you make it in, we assume that you have something to contribute. And that makes everyone curious about your perspective. We want to find out what you have to offer. If you are a Facebook engineer, you are trusted."

Everything at Facebook is built to reinforce a culture of social interaction, from the physical layout of the campus to the way employees are onboarded. These features ensure a social atmosphere that stretches across the company.

There are also social elements particular to the engineering department.

Facebook's enormous codebase is deliberately structured as one big file system, where an infrastructure team can see the code of the Newsfeed team, and the Payments team can see the code for the Groups team. This code management strategy is called a "monolithic repository."

A monolithic repository allows teams to view each other's codebases, leave comments, and make API improvements. "The fact that any piece of code that you wrote would be visible to everybody created an environment of transparency, which I think is healthy," says Arturo. "The software you write should be public. If you write code that you don't want other engineers to see, then there's probably not a great reason for that."

The monolithic codebase has both technical and cultural advantages.

At Facebook, if an engineer on one team sees a bug in the codebase of another team, that engineer has the freedom to fix the bug. This contrasts with most companies, where an individual's responsibility is localized to their specific team.

Large companies are often broken down into small, rigid teams, because it is easier to reason about your task when you are not exposed to the entire organization.

A large software company is tremendously complex, so most are managed like a pyramid, with teams at the bottom. These teams keep engineers in their team silos, with managers and directors forming the connective tissue between higher-level components of an organization.

Companies can be successful with this siloed, partitioned operating model. But Facebook works differently.

There is a poster at Facebook that says, "Nothing at Facebook is somebody else's problem." At Facebook, company cohesion takes precedence over individual teams. Engineering silos are reduced by allowing everyone access to the same monolithic codebase. Every individual can think holistically about the overall Facebook product.

Facebook encourages knowledge sharing and collaboration between departments.

For example, Facebook has content moderation teams and engineers who build software to make the content moderators more effective. To empathize with these moderators and understand their problems firsthand, an engineer working on content moderation software can embed in the content moderation team and use that software. By using the moderation tools they are working on, the engineers can understand the pain points that other departments experience.

Facebook's social cohesion is not a product of any specific internal decision. Social cohesion comes from thinking about how every facet of the company's operations could affect interpersonal dynamics.

Importantly, the goal is not to create a monoculture within Facebook. The goal is to create a sense of shared ownership that emerges throughout the company. Shared ownership means that your responsibilities extend beyond your team. Shared ownership also means that people on other teams will have your back when something goes wrong.

In the highly creative, dynamic field of modern software engineering, social skills can provide massive leverage. Facebook hires employees who can communicate with each other and gives them the tools they need to build strong social ties.

# 9

# CODE WINS ARGUMENTS

*"We used to say code wins arguments. That was a culture we tried to maintain, and it served us well."*

—NICK SCHROCK

A modern trope of software engineering is the idea of the "10x engineer."

A 10x engineer is someone who has ten times the impact of an average engineer. Some engineers believe that the "10x engineer" is a myth. But most experienced engineers I have spoken to agree that 10x engineering is a real phenomenon. And while these 10x engineers almost always come with extreme personality quirks, most managers will say that if given the choice, they will take a 10x engineer over an average engineer any day.

Nick Schrock is serious about software engineering. His default expression is one of intense focus, whether he is looking at a whiteboard diagram or looking directly into your eyes, his brain processing your words with scrutiny. Nick's flair of stylish blonde hair belies the disposition of a football coach: gruff, tough, and unafraid to give you the cold hard truth.

"Engineering is a creative endeavor. And like any creative endeavor, there is a huge, wide dynamic range of capability," says Nick. "The mythical 10x engineer is not a myth. I think there are 10x engineers, and those 10x engineers naturally become influential. These people understand the needs of the other developers. They build infrastructure that other developers can then use to be productive, and this causes a multiplier effect. Engineers are often 10x because they are leveling up the other engineers through their code."

Not only does Nick believe in the 10x engineer—he believes in something else: the influencer engineer.

"The influencers within the company are not Instagram models. The influencers are the engineers who actually write important code. Through their code, their actions, and their discussions, these engineers can convince other people to do stuff. They are influencer engineers."

When Nick was a young engineer, he studied the behavior of the senior engineers. "I would interact with them and respond to their advocacy. I began to understand how these engineers affect change. I learned how they became influential."

So how does a normal engineer become an influencer engineer? The answer is simple: code wins arguments.

Code is indisputable. When an engineer wants to prove something technical, they can make their point by solving a problem with code or creating a useful abstraction. Code is a shareable artifact. Public code review makes it easy to tell who is making the smart engineering decisions.

Influence is built through reputation, and code commit history is an unambiguous measure of reputation.

Facebook's internal code management tool reveals that the engineers who write the most influential code end up communicating the most across the company. These engineers naturally become influencers.

An influencer engineer solves technical problems and affects organizational change. So, what can a company do to foster influencer engineers?

Arturo Bejar gives the manager's perspective. "Facebook tries to create an environment where anyone can feel empowered to tackle large problems, even if they are brand new to the company. When you come out of boot camp, you are given enough problem space to work on to demonstrate your maximum capabilities. If you try and fail, that's OK."

At some companies, it takes years to earn the right to work on something interesting. But Facebook gives engineers room to be ambitious, regardless of their skill level.

As a manager at Facebook, Arturo saw many engineers develop their skills rapidly. "When you give engineers a big chance to prove themselves, you can get really strong engineers really fast. You give them freedom, you give them responsibility, and you give them feedback."

A hungry engineer can choose to rise to the level of responsibility they've been given. They can choose to respond well to coaching. If they do, they can have an impact. And an engineer who has impact can become an influencer.

Influencer engineers not only build new software. They evangelize how to use that software within the company. Influencer engineers can spread their ideas in different ways. Some influencer engineers do public speaking within the company, while some write documentation or internal blog posts.

A clique will form around an influencer engineer. Influencers can win over the hearts and minds of other engineers, single-handedly changing the technical direction of a company for better or worse.

In some problematic cases, the influencer engineer can undermine the efforts of their manager.

Arturo Bejar describes the problem of dealing with a talented engineer who is causing organizational friction. "At Facebook, we wanted all the engineers to feel connected. When an engineer is talented, but they are causing conflict, then you have to help them change their behavior. Otherwise, they need to find a different job."

But what if the engineer is critical to the success of the company? What if the engineer is a "brilliant jerk?" Is there a way to retain an influencer engineer whose influence is negative?

Arturo sighs, perhaps remembering the difficult choices he had to make as a manager at Facebook. "You can try to isolate the engineer and surround them only with the people that can tolerate them. But we couldn't do this at Facebook. The company is built around close connections across engineering. Isolating brilliant engineers that cause collateral damage is a management mistake."

In the ideal engineering culture, an influencer engineer should be able to thrive.

If the engineer wants to lead, they should have opportunities to lead. If the engineer is junior, they might have raw talent but need some guidance, and their manager should help them identify goals to work towards. A talented senior engineer might have a particular kind of work they like to do and should be placed in an environment that accommodates their preferences.

At Facebook, code wins arguments. Sometimes, an influencer engineer creates too many arguments. These engineers cannot be allowed to disrupt a positive culture. To give them a chance for self-examination, it can be helpful to collect anonymous feedback from their peers. Once this influencer engineer can see the way that others perceive them, they will hopefully wake up to the consequences of an abrasive attitude.

In the worst case, in order to maintain the delicate balance between individualism and social cohesion, it may be necessary to remove the influencer engineer from the company.

# PART 3

# TECHNOLOGY

# 10

# CROSS-PLATFORM

*"Strategic inflection points are about fundamental change in any business, technological or not."*

—ANDY GROVE, ONLY THE PARANOID SURVIVE

Facebook began as a browser-based web application. When its core business model of desktop advertising was threatened by the consumer trend towards mobile, Facebook spent four years evolving into a mobile company.

To make this shift, Facebook had to learn to build products across both mobile and desktop—two environments with very different usage patterns. This evolution required a change in both software engineering and product development.

Facebook's first attempt at a pivot to mobile was a browser-based HTML5 application.

While this looks like a poor decision in retrospect, it seemed sensible at the time. Facebook assumed that mobile users would be mostly using their mobile browsers, rather than native mobile apps. After all, this was a time when email preferences had shifted from desktop-based Outlook to browser-based Gmail. Document editing had shifted from desktop-based Microsoft Word to browser-based Google Docs.

At the time, it seemed like everything could move from desktop applications to the browser. Perhaps HTML5 would improve so rapidly that native mobile platforms would become displaced by the power of the web.

Lee Byron is a thin, bespectacled web developer. He looks like someone who belongs in a coffee shop, sipping black espresso as he struggles with Chrome debugging tools on a tiny laptop screen.

Lee is the late-stage evolutionary form of the primordial coffee shop engineers. These hipster developers cut their teeth in the early 2010s, tinkering with PHP, struggling with iQuery, and enduring the pains of the primitive two-way data binding of Backbone.js.

For many years, the frontend was an afterthought, playing second fiddle to the backend engineers doing Real Computer Science. By 2010, the software industry understood that the frontend was critically important. JavaScript, the language of the web, was here to stay, and the hipster developers who could speak it went from wallflowers to central planners of the future of software.

In college, Lee had not spent any time studying computer science. Instead he'd focused on industrial design and human-computer interaction. At Facebook, he found his way into mobile design, and discovered that he also knew enough about engineering to be productive.

Facebook knew the importance of the web and the power of JavaScript before the rest of the industry did. When the company placed its incorrect bet on HTML5, it was basing its decision on an anticipated dynamic between the web and mobile devices. Lee Byron provides the historical perspective.

"Our early bet was that Apple and Google would compete to have higher quality mobile browsers. Steve Jobs was describing the iPhone as a portal to the web. And the web was a great, open platform. It also happened to be Facebook's bread-and-butter. Our core expertise."

Browser technology did not turn out to be the center of the mobile universe. Mobile browsers were stagnating, with Safari and Chrome becoming buggy and crash-prone and falling short of the standards of desktop web browsers.

Instead of the browser, the app was the center of the mobile universe, and Android and iOS developed substantially different operating systems on which to run those apps. Both mobile environments had native APIs that required developers to be aware of which device they were coding for. A browser-based approach with the same codebase for both iOS and Android could not be as performant as individual apps built for the Android and iOS native platforms.

Facebook realized that an entire mobile rewrite was needed for the client devices. The new mobile applications would need to be small enough to fit on a phone and powerful enough to drive an experience that matched the desktop version.

The networking software that routed information to client devices would also need to be rearchitected. Facebook was realizing that the cellular connection was not fast enough to deliver information as efficiently as the desktop connections could.

The new world of mobile placed constraints across the Facebook engineering process. Facebook was forced to rethink its entire application, says Lee Byron.

"Facebook does so many different things. It is a huge application. So what do you put on the server, and what do you put on the client? When we were working on the desktop, we never had to think about this question. In the desktop web, all the business logic happens on the server, because the network is fast enough. The network between internal services and databases is fast enough. But on the mobile apps, all the business logic needs to be on the client in order to be snappy and responsive. And that meant the mobile app needed to be many, many megabytes large."

The mobile app environment forced Facebook to push lots of functionality into a constrained application size. Facebook was constrained by the network as well as the limited memory that mobile platforms provide app developers. "We constantly rode the edge of what the biggest application could be," says Lee.

"Apple told us that Facebook was not only the biggest app in the iOS App Store market. It was bigger than any internal apps at Apple, and that included Springboard, which is the equivalent to Finder on the Mac. We were bigger than the entire file system UI for iOS. So it was very difficult to get the Facebook app to load correctly on iOS."

"Every week, our release engineers complained that we were moments away from not being able to download from the app store or boot on a device. But through some amount of magic, infrastructure improvements, constant cleanup, and Apple making this limit a moving and growing target, we rarely actually couldn't ship the app. But we did always ride that edge."

Facebook's existential jump into mobile caused the company to push the boundaries of modern application development.

As it became a cross-platform application, Facebook was forced to operate with high performance in a constrained environment. Mobile applications have finite battery power, limited cellular network connectivity, and a small memory allocation. In addition, mobile apps need to be compatible with the wide range of operating systems to which they can be deployed. Old phones need to work with new versions of Facebook.

Although the shift to mobile was a painful one, Facebook dealt with it as swiftly as possible. Every company is handicapped by the necessities of mobile. Facebook built internal processes, tools, and institutions that minimized the ongoing pain associated with mobile development.

In retrospect, the struggle to become cross-platform has given Facebook a strong competitive advantage that it would not otherwise have.

The platform shift to mobile forced Facebook to develop a completely new set of core competencies. Mobile changed nearly everything about how Facebook develops software, from product design to release engineering.

# RELEASE ENGINEERING

*"We're moving fast. When we release software so fast, things might go wrong, but we can fix them quickly. We can react quickly. We can develop quickly. We can do product releases quickly. That's the main difference I found from previous places to Facebook."*

—CHUCK ROSSI, FACEBOOK DIRECTOR OF
RELEASE ENGINEERING FROM 2008 TO 2018

Release engineering is the process by which software is released to users.

Software starts as raw code. That code is compiled into executable files, then bundled into artifacts that can be easily ported from one machine to another. Finally, it is deployed to the target machine, where it runs.

As software is being released, it moves through a series of testing environments. Developers study the software using simulated inputs in order to discover bugs before the software makes it to the end of the release process.

When Chuck Rossi joined Facebook in 2008, he was the most experienced release engineer at the company. For the previous twenty years, Chuck had been working in software non-stop, and consistently at the most highly regarded companies. IBM, NetGravity, Silicon Graphics, VMware, Google, Facebook: Chuck's resume tracks a steady timeline of engineering excellence.

Now in his early fifties, Chuck is a grizzled veteran of the software industry. With his beliefs in government service, gun rights, and national defense, Chuck is a counterexample to the popular meme that tech companies are overrun by a left-leaning monoculture. Chuck is bearded, well-dressed, and uniquely opinionated.

Chuck thinks for himself, viewing every situation with fresh eyes—which is exactly what Facebook needed out of its director of release engineering at the time he joined the company.

"When I came into the company, I was faced with a decision," says Chuck. "I had twenty years of experience when I joined Facebook. I had worked at VMware, and Google, and IBM, and the way that these crazy kids were releasing software was like nothing I had ever seen. I had to decide: was I going to lay down the law and bring in those best practices that I learned at Google? Or was I going to go with this organic new thing?"

Chuck began to explore the engineering practices of Facebook. He was surprised, confused, and impressed by the release engineering system that he encountered.

"Facebook was always in motion. It was always on the brink of disaster. But it was always given 100 percent attention. When I was at Google, it was all about stability. At Facebook, I learned that there was a cost to enforcing that stability. Facebook was a different mindset. The 'move fast' mindset."

Chuck observed that releasing so much software per day caused more bugs than he had seen at his previous employers. But the fast pace also enabled developers to fix those bugs faster than any other companies could fix theirs.

Release engineering is closely tied to the practice of automated software testing. Software testing takes several different forms: unit tests, integration tests, smoke tests, end-to-end tests. Every test provides a small layer of insurance that a piece of software works the way that the developer intended.

Software testing is crucial to an effective release process.

During a release, a new piece of code is subjected to all of the tests that have been written. If no tests have been written, then there are only minimal guarantees that the software will work as expected.

Automated tests guarantee the quality of the software you are releasing. But the downside is that writing tests takes time. If you spend time writing tests, you are sacrificing time that could be spent building new features—which means your product is developing more slowly.

Through 2009, there were zero unit tests at Facebook.

When a new feature was built, the developer tested it on their local machine manually. After clicking around the interface and making sure everything worked as expected, the developer pushed the code to production. Most of the time, that would work fine.

But occasionally, a developer would forget to manually test something, and the production code would break. As Facebook hired more developers, this started happening more frequently. Without any unit tests, it was hard for all the developers to keep the code base clean.

Eventually, the lack of tests crippled Facebook's pace of

development. New constraints were imposed upon the release process, as Facebook adopted a style of software engineering called Test-Driven Development.

"You wrote your unit tests with your code," says Chuck Rossi. "If you didn't have tests when you delivered your code, you were flagged. The code delivery tools promoted a culture of testing."

With the right testing practices in place, Facebook's software releases stabilized. But some developers still had a tendency to be careless. When software was insufficiently tested, it could cause problems in production.

To improve the social norms of the release process, Facebook code management tooling was imbued with social networking elements over time.

One feature was "Push Karma," a four-star rating system that tracked how responsible individual developers were in their management of software releases. Push Karma allowed developers to issue a demerit if another developer poorly handled the release of their software. If a developer pushed code, then went missing in action when the code landed in production, that was something that the release team wanted to remember. A developer with bad karma developed a bad reputation.

Push Karma helped prod developers to take ownership over their release processes. Chuck describes Push Karma as an important system, and one that is managed delicately. Everyone makes mistakes, and sometimes those mistakes cause production errors. Push Karma is just a soft reminder, not a strict social credit score.

Over time, Facebook's release process has become more sophisticated.

Today, when a developer submits a pull request, a risk profile is automatically generated for the software release. That risk profile takes into account a set of factors including what files were touched, who pushed the code, and what the downstream effects of the pull request could potentially be.

In an environment where so much code is being pushed, this risk profile provides a gauge that can help the release engineering team watch a new commit more closely.

But for all of the sophistication in Facebook's release tooling, everything changed in 2011, as Facebook started to build native iOS and Android apps.

After moving to mobile, the Facebook product no longer revolved around the simplicity of the desktop. Facebook had to test its mobile app across multiple versions of iOS and multiple pieces of iPhone hardware. For Android, it was even worse, as there was a wide spectrum of hardware vendors.

But the most painful part of releasing to mobile was the manual app store review process.

Every release to mobile is bottlenecked by Apple and Google. If you want to release software to the iPhone, you must go through the manual review process on the Apple App Store. If you want to release software to Android, you must go through the manual review process on the Google Play Store.

Manual app review dramatically slows down mobile app development, because every new software build must be downloaded, manually tested, and approved by a human reviewer.

The benefit of manual review is that the human reviewers are able to find crashes, bugs, memory leaks, and exploitative apps.

The downside is that manual review makes it impossible for developers to issue quick fixes for small bugs. A software release will often ship with small bugs that are discovered and reported by the user base. For browser-based apps, fixing a bug like this is simple and fast. There is no manual review. But in the mobile app world, even a tiny bug fix must be scrutinized by a human reviewer.

To understand the pains of the manual review process, let's take a quick historical review of the software release process.

In the 1990s, software was printed onto CDs. Consumers purchased these CDs and installed software on their computers. In the 2000s, improved Internet bandwidth caused an increasing number of users to download software from the Internet and install it. More recently, the improved performance of browsers and mobile networks has allowed us to load and run entire applications in our browser instantly. An application as complicated as Facebook can be accessed by simply visiting Facebook.com in a browser.

As the consumption of software has changed, the software release process has changed with it. When software was printed onto CDs, there was very little room for error. If your software company printed 100,000 CDs with a piece of software that had a bug, it could cause your company to go bankrupt.

Today, software is released and consumed over the Internet. If you accidentally release a piece of software with a bug, you should be able to instantly fix it and push your new software out to your users. As a result, the pace of software development has improved dramatically.

Web development is an environment with few constraints for what software can be deployed and consumed. The mobile app ecosystem is different. The mobile app ecosystem is mostly managed by Google and Apple. Android applications are installed using the Google Play store, and iPhone applications are installed using Apple's App Store.

The app store human review process is intended to be a barrier to poorly written or malicious software. And the human reviewers really do catch significant problems. But there is a significant cost to this human review.

Slowing down the mobile release process prevents developers from pushing out new code quickly, and if you can't push code out quickly, then you can't fix known problems quickly.

Chuck Rossi reflects soberly on the state of mobile software releases. "You won't find a single mobile developer who is a fan of the mobile release process. When Facebook went to mobile, we were forced to change. We were forced to give up what we had learned about how to build software safely. It was like going back in time, to have these ridiculous handcuffs placed on you by the app stores."

In 2011, Facebook needed a strategy for reliably making it through the mobile review process. They needed to avoid small bugs, because every small bug would lead to a new release with the bug fix, and another slow manual review.

In order to ensure that Facebook's app would be approved by the app stores, the company scheduled its mobile releases on two-four week periods so that there could be time dedicated to bug fixing and final preparations before app store submissions. Eventually Facebook settled on releasing the biggest mobile apps every week. This was in stark contrast to the Facebook web app, which was pushing multiple releases every day.

Chuck Rossi remembers the difficulty of having to slow down Facebook's release process. "We had a tough time," sighs Chuck. "We were going from a world of desktop web, where we had total control, where we could release every thirty seconds or every thirty days, where we could do it safely and correctly. We went to mobile, and we were forced into this world of old-style enterprise release."

When Chuck left Facebook, the company's mobile app portfolio included Facebook, Messenger, WhatsApp, and Instagram. Chuck's mobile app releases involved four of the top ten apps in the world.

"I had the biggest user base of mobile users in the world across all those apps. It was the most terrifying thing to take 10,000 new code changes, package it into a bullet, fire that bullet at the horizon and that bullet, once it leaves the barrel, it's gone. I cannot get it back. I can't fix it. That fundamental model is terrifying in effect."

Errors will inevitably occur in the software release process. And in the mobile app ecosystem, it is impossible to quickly fix these errors. The software developer must wait for the manual review team to approve the new build.

Chuck Rossi is highly attentive and serious about his job. But even he was capable of making errors. "One time I released the wrong app icon for the Facebook app. How many hundreds of millions of phones got Facebook with this incorrect placeholder for the app icon? I guarantee you, there is still a phone out there from 2016 that has this app on it with the wrong icon."

Facebook is not the only company that has struggled to develop to an efficient mobile release process. I asked Chuck what other companies should do in order to optimize their mobile workflows.

"My advice is to make your release process a first-class citizen. Use the right tools, allocate the right budget, and hire the right people to make this part of your culture. Specifically, keep your release processes as quick as possible. Small, manageable, quick releases can be quite scalable and quite beneficial. Small, discrete changes will keep you agile. They are much easier to review. They are easier to manage."

Based on his time at Facebook, Chuck encourages mobile developers to get to a one-week release cycle.

"Your core product needs to be released every week on mobile. It will let you keep your app alive. It will let you keep your sanity. If you don't think you can, you should try. If you force yourself to move faster, you will flush out all the things that need to be fixed."

Chuck has every reason to be proud of a one-week release cycle on mobile. But this release cadence is so much slower than the permissionless release process of the web. Chuck acknowledges the limitations that come from being hamstrung by the major mobile platforms. "There were epic battles between us and Apple and Google," he says. "But there was only so much we could do."

Over time, Facebook has been able to reclaim some of the agility of its web-based release process by investing heavily in key technologies.

React Native is a system for dynamically changing mobile applications by delivering JavaScript code over the network. This allows developers to release new software to mobile applications without going through the manual review process.

Another tool Facebook uses to enable more dynamic software releases is feature flagging. Feature flagging allows Facebook employees to turn software features on and off without doing an entire software release. The Facebook mobile apps are released with a large volume of code that is deactivated for most users. Facebook can remotely activate that code after testing it safely on small sub-groups of Facebook users without affecting the entire Facebook user base.

Both of these tools can be used outside of Facebook. React Native is an open source library, and feature flagging has spread to a number of software companies.

Chuck Rossi left Facebook in 2018 after more than a decade with the company. "I miss being in the middle of it and providing that conduit to make sure it's done safely, correctly and for the benefit of the customers," he says.

"Software lives and breathes. My role is to keep this software living and breathing, and getting it out to the customers."

# NETWORKING

"*When Facebook introduced mobile, there were a ton of constraints on the infrastructure. There were constraints from the frontend to the backend, to the release process, to how we talk to the network. Mobile introduced problems that were completely new to Facebook as an engineering and a product organization.*"

—LEE BYRON, FORMER FACEBOOK ENGINEER

Facebook is a large social graph with heavy user interactivity and numerous backend data sources.

Since its early days, Facebook has placed unprecedented demands on the user's web browser. With the expansion to mobile, these performance demands became even more severe.

Facebook is very data intensive. Consider the newsfeed. There are hundreds of objects in your newsfeed. Some of these objects are videos. Some of them are large blocks of text. Some objects have hundreds of other nested elements, including comments, likes, emojis, gifs, and other responses.

On a desktop computer, the Facebook app can be greedy, and fetch all of these objects from the backend with no concern for the amount of bandwidth required. But on mobile, bandwidth is more restricted. The mobile Facebook app might not want to fetch the data for every object ahead of time.

Fetching items for a mobile newsfeed poses a complicated networking problem.

Mobile users with low bandwidth scroll through a newsfeed full of high-dimensional objects. An object in a newsfeed might be a photo that your friend has posted. That photo could include hundreds of nested objects beneath it: comments, likes, emojis, gifs, and other responses. On the backend, the data model includes each of these fields.

However, the mobile client does not require all of these fields. If I am looking at the photo on a mobile client such as the Facebook iPhone app, my mobile client does not need to immediately fetch the photo as well as all of the nested objects beneath it. I might only want to read the top two-three comments. Or I might scroll past the photo and only see its likes and reactions.

If I engage with the photo, or pause my scrolling, my phone should realize that and fetch the additional data from the backend. My phone should prepare for me to click the photo and read lots of comments.

A developer working on the Facebook client has to program the functionality to choose which parts of an object to request from the backend. When Facebook was built for the desktop, this fetching logic was the backend developer's responsibility, while the frontend developer did not have control over what to fetch.

Over time, the Facebook data model became more heterogeneous. Objects in the database backend became bigger. The range of mobile clients and user bandwidth levels also increased as Facebook expanded into more international markets with sparse cellular connectivity.

Lee Byron recalls the problems that Facebook started to see as mobile development matured.

"When we moved to mobile web, we started to interact with 3G networks. 3G networks have poor upload and download speeds, but the real pain point is latency. When you want to make a connection, the latency can often be over an entire second. In the worst case, it might take thirty seconds to load a page. And that's just for loading a webpage where you are downloading HTML, and maybe a couple of JavaScript files."

As Facebook's mobile applications became more sophisticated, the performance got even worse because more networking logic was being shifted into the mobile client. The number of network requests increased, and they all had to go out over the cellular network.

Facebook struggled to find the balance between logic on the client-side and on the server-side.

Different frontend clients have different constraints on how much data they ideally accept from a backend request. A request for more data requires more bandwidth but gives the frontend client a lot to display to the user. A request for less data can be accomplished over less bandwidth but might require the client to make additional requests to fetch subsequent pieces of data.

The ideal request pattern would fetch exactly the right amount of data needed at a given time.

"The main struggle was around newsfeed. We wanted a way to get all the information that we would need for a newsfeed object in a single network request."

It became clear that Facebook could not operate on mobile

with the same networking tools it had used for desktop. Lee Byron, Nick Schrock, and a third engineer named Dan Schafer decided to take a step back and think through their options.

Lee, Nick, and Dan had each spent years at Facebook. They had an intimate understanding of how data flowed through the system. Over the course of several months, the three of them spent hours huddled around laptop screens and sketching code on whiteboards. Eventually, they arrived at a solution: GraphQL.

GraphQL is a middleware server that accepts JSON-like query requests and federates those queries to backend database servers. It simplifies client request logic by moving code out of the client.

Thanks to GraphQL queries, a client can specify exactly the data it needs from the backend. The response payload size stays minimal, and there are fewer round trips over a slow network.

When Facebook was on the verge of its IPO and struggling through its transition to mobile, GraphQL provided a sorely needed performance boost for the site's mobile users. "We figured it out just in time," says Lee. "That shift between platforms has killed other companies. It came very close to killing Facebook."

GraphQL didn't just improve the request latency of mobile data fetching. It had a profound impact on the entire application development workflow.

GraphQL decouples backend infrastructure developers from frontend clients. The backend developer is required to spin up a GraphQL server and define a GraphQL schema, which outlines the data model that can be queried. Then, frontend developers for any client device can specify the data they want from this GraphQL server.

In a world before GraphQL, a custom server endpoint was needed to respond to any particular kind of request. With GraphQL, the query language is flexible enough to satisfy a wide range of queries. The same GraphQL server endpoint can satisfy the queries for different users.

Facebook open sourced GraphQL in 2015, and it has been widely adopted across the industry. As time goes on, more and more companies have the highly interactive mobile interfaces and complex data fetching infrastructure that Facebook grappled with early on.

From the business model to the frontend to the backend: the shift in consumer preferences towards mobile has impacted every consumer company at every layer of the stack. GraphQL is a novel solution to the networking constraints that were placed on mobile frontend developers.

# RETHINKING BEST PRACTICES

*"I see this place, it's crazy, it looks like a clown show and yet, things are working really well."*

—KENT BECK, FORMER FACEBOOK ENGINEER

Facebook's engineering organization is truly one-of-a-kind. I don't mean that as an unambiguous compliment to the company, I mean it as an objective observation. In my conversations with senior Facebook engineers and managers, they readily acknowledged that Facebook is like an alien civilization relative to the average big tech company. A common self-deprecating term that many Facebook engineers use is "clown show," as if Facebook is like a goofy carnival full of engineers too stupid to see their own mistakes.

From its earliest interactions with the outside world, Facebook's engineering department was not well-understood by the broader software engineering community.

Software engineering has its roots in academic computer science, where ideas are justified with formal proofs. The engineering practices of IBM, Microsoft, and Google have a streak of mathematical rigor. Senior engineers at these companies are treated with the reverence of tenured university professors. Building an operating system or a search engine is serious business, only to be done by serious engineers.

Comparatively, the early Facebook organization was indeed a clown show, a hacker collective that produced buggy software for teenagers.

In the early days, when a Facebook engineer attended a tech conference and gave a talk about how the company developed its software, the reaction from the external engineering world was that Facebook was some kind of silly joke, a shoddy PHP application run by a bunch of college kids who got lucky with their website but didn't know how to do serious computer science.

Over time, the engineering world has learned to take Facebook seriously.

Facebook has made unconventional decisions, but there are good reasons for each of those decisions. The circumstances under which Facebook evolved have given it a set of strengths and weaknesses that are hard to comprehend if you don't have a holistic picture of the company and its history.

Looking at Facebook's infrastructure is like looking at the creatures that live in steam vents at the bottom of the ocean: a bizarre, yet thriving ecosystem borne of unique evolutionary fate.

As the Facebook product came to market, users wanted new features faster than Facebook could build them. Facebook hired the best engineers it could find and tasked them with building new functionality as fast as possible. These engineers were hackers—the type of programmers who had grown up spending their nights and weekends building games, chat systems, and crude artificial intelligence applications.

The early Facebook engineering team was young, confident, and eager to build new features and see how the world would interact with them. New features were developed at the cost of testing the existing product, and when the new features were pushed to production, they would sometimes cause bugs, or complete outages of the Facebook platform.

But the benefits of this fast product development were numerous. Users loved the rapid evolution of the product, and Facebook was in the unique position of releasing popular but not super important software.

As late as 2010, Facebook was not yet a crucial piece of communications infrastructure for everyone's daily life. It wasn't an operating system, or a heart rate monitor, or an embedded temperature control chip.

Facebook was free software, and it was not used for life-or-death situations. It was used for making friends, sending messages, planning events, and sharing cool links. If Facebook went down every once in a while, it wasn't the end of the world. Facebook moved fast, and things were occasionally broken. Facebook did not need to build software at the glacial pace of an enterprise product company.

Kent Beck entered into this strange organization in 2011.

Kent Beck is a legendary figure in the world of software engineering. As an early advocate of Test-Driven Development (TDD), Kent popularized the idea of writing unit tests before writing code that would satisfy those tests. A unit test isolates and tests a small piece of functionality within a large piece of software. Practitioners of Test-Driven Development write tens or hundreds of tests in order to simulate the many cases that could potentially occur within their software. Test-Driven Development helps maintain the quality of a codebase.

Kent Beck is the author of nine books, including "Extreme Programming Explained" and "Test-Driven Development by Example." Kent's methods are so widely accepted throughout the industry that one of my instructors in college mandated that all of our software engineering assignments were written using the Test-Driven Development process.

When Kent Beck joined Facebook in 2011, he was fifty years old and thought he had seen everything in the software industry. During Facebook Bootcamp, Kent started to realize that Facebook was different from any other company he had been a part of. "I had a huge case of imposter syndrome when I joined the company," says Kent. "Even though I had been in the industry for a long time, I realized just how different everything was at Facebook."

After graduating from bootcamp, Kent began to explore Facebook's codebase and culture. He was shocked by what he saw.

Across the Facebook organization, there was vast experimentation. It was a factory of innovation, with engineers constantly prototyping new products and testing new internal tools. The massive scale of the user base allowed

Facebook to think about product development in a way no company before it had been able to, and the volume of data allowed Facebook to accurately validate its new products as it decided how to invest its resources.

"Facebook's style was really good at exploring new engines of growth. You have very little to lose in that moment," says Kent Beck. "This is where move fast and break things is exactly the right attitude to take. If you have nothing to lose, breaking something has no cost, so just go for it. I call that the exploration phase. You want to place as many bets as possible, because you can't analyze your way to success."

With so many opportunities to take advantage of, Facebook engineers were sometimes spread thin. Even small teams would work on big features, which would deliver value to millions of users.

Facebook engineers did not always have the bandwidth to unit test these new features. Engineers could run tests in a simulated environment, then do a small rollout of the feature to 1 percent of a real user base. If it worked with the 1 percent of the user base, the engineers could gradually ramp up to 100 percent of the user base.

Rather than unit testing every single new feature, Facebook engineers had the autonomy to decide when to spend time writing unit tests. If a feature became popular, engineers could always add more tests later.

As an advocate of the steady process of Test-Driven Development, Kent Beck could hardly believe how stable Facebook's software was despite such limited testing. "They weren't doing the things in my books. But they weren't failing. I'm OK with people doing things differently than in my books; I just want them to fail," Beck jokes.

As Kent Beck became more familiar with how Facebook worked, he realized that he wasn't just learning something new about Facebook; he was learning something new about software engineering.

"Every software process has to be shaped by context," says Kent. "Facebook's context was unique. They were exploring two things simultaneously: the space of what social media interaction looked like, as well as all the difficult engineering problems that were associated with social networking."

At Facebook, Kent realized that he needed to rethink many of his long-held beliefs about how to build software. "We can write useful stories about the software development process, but they're stories, they're not recipes."

Why should different companies have different testing practices? Consider Facebook in contrast with Microsoft.

As the dominant software company through the 1990s, Microsoft defined many of the modern best practices of software engineering. Considering that Microsoft sells an operating system that runs a large percentage of the world's computers, it's no surprise that the company is extremely careful with its software testing and release process.

Microsoft's delicate approach has been evangelized throughout the industry, and many enterprise software companies have followed the best practices of Microsoft to great success. But the release process of modern web-based software looks remarkably different than the '90s world of Microsoft Windows, delivered via CD.

In the world of web-based software, it is much easier to issue a bug fix than in the world of software distributed via CDs. The developer pushes a new version out to the server, and the user automatically loads the new version on their browser or mobile app. Consequently, it is less costly to release software that has a bug.

Of course, there is a delicate balance. A company never wants to release software that permanently corrupts the database or software that causes users to distrust the company. Some parts of a codebase are extremely sensitive, while other parts can tolerate rapid iteration.

If a codebase can tolerate rapid iteration and fewer tests,

then the company should probably be rapidly iterating and writing fewer tests. The cost of testing too much and moving too slowly can be severe.

In its early days, Facebook's rapid pace of development was jarring for engineers accustomed to how other companies built software.

When Nick Schrock joined Facebook in 2009, he had worked at Microsoft for a year. Microsoft builds mission-critical business software, and Nick understood the Microsoft way of deliberate testing. Shortly after joining Facebook, he realized that he was looking at something starkly different from anything he had seen at Microsoft.

"I was shocked at the way Facebook did engineering," says Nick. "And then I was amazed. Maybe amazed and appalled simultaneously. The thing I was amazed by was the bias towards velocity. I had never worked in an environment like that." When Nick was at Microsoft, the software was built much slower.

"Right after I joined Facebook, I was expected to commit code during my first day on the job. That code would be released to production every single Tuesday. I had never worked in an environment like that. It felt unnatural at first, but when I got used to it, the release process felt extraordinarily liberating. Facebook decided to have a fast release cycle, and the company was forced to build infrastructure around that."

There was a cost to this rapid pace of engineering. In some places, Facebook's software was a big jumble of spaghetti code that was barely maintainable. "When I hopped into a particular file in the PHP code base, I would lose the healthy color of my skin," says Nick. "It sounds ironic, but it was a testament to the overall quality of the engineers that they were able to be productive in such a hostile environment."

Nick learned to thrive while moving at the fast pace of Facebook engineering. But as he explains, some new Facebook engineers never get used to the way the company works. "There are talented, brilliant engineers who come into Facebook and then churn out quickly. They would be very successful at other companies. But they can't deal with the level of controlled chaos that occurred within Facebook."

One of the most acute sources of chaos that Nick encountered was the lack of tests. After working at Microsoft, Nick was surprised that Facebook could succeed for so long without developing a concerted strategy for testing. "When I joined, I was engineer number 180. The company was five years old. We had 200 million active daily users. And there were zero tests in the codebase. Zero."

Nick's reaction was similar to that of Chuck Rossi, the

release engineering veteran who joined Facebook to fix its process of software delivery. It was natural to be astounded that Facebook had become a juggernaut of a company despite lacking any unit testing processes.

As surprising as it was, Facebook continued to hum along for many years without systematic testing. But shortly after Nick joined the company, the total lack of tests started to become a problem.

"We were just pushing a lot of bugs to production. Users were encountering those bugs, and it was causing a bad experience," says Nick. "We were starting to hire more experienced engineers. These were not engineers coming out of college but experienced engineers from places like Microsoft and Google. And the feedback those engineers would give to the leadership was always consistent: we need more tests. These experienced engineers understood what made Facebook successful, but they were still being blunt about this need for tests. And to their credit, Facebook leadership understood this as well."

Facebook began implementing many more tests throughout software infrastructure. Nick Schrock recalls this change of pace, and the interactions between engineers and the management team.

"Every engineering organization needs to decide how much

time they're going to spend cutting down the trees and how much time they're going to spend sharpening their saws. Facebook had spent many years cutting down trees, and now it was time to sharpen their saws."

Since Nick joined Facebook, it has evolved from an organization with zero unit tests to one with a healthy measure of testing. In 2020, Facebook relies heavily on test-driven development.

Facebook's aggressive strategy of building new functionality rather than reinforcing existing features was not the company's only unconventional choice. Facebook has always been willing to make engineering decisions that run contrary to traditional software engineering methods.

Facebook's backend was built with PHP, a language that has been ridiculed by software engineers for decades. The frontend runs on ReactJS, a framework that was initially scoffed at for its blending of JavaScript and HTML into the bizarre file format JSX. Facebook's networking was redefined by GraphQL, a data fetching protocol that supplants REST.

Nick Schrock has a strong understanding of computer science theory and a healthy respect for time-tested software engineering principles. But during his time at Facebook, he repeatedly saw things that made him question the established wisdom.

Facebook open sourced React and GraphQL, which Nick co-created. After they were made available to the public, both projects were criticized on Twitter. He recalls his favorite tweet.

"Someone in a critical way tweeted, 'Facebook: rethinking best practices.' Nick's eyes twinkle as he smiles. "It was not an approving tweet, but we were like, 'Yup! That's exactly what we're doing. We maintain the beginner's mentality. We try to strip away previous orthodoxy and try to approach problems from first principles. When you combine that with the unique problems that Facebook was trying to solve, plus the personalities and capabilities of the engineers at Facebook, it was a magical mix."

In some cases, rethinking best practices has led to Facebook redefining best practices. Facebook's open source projects have been widely adopted as solutions to recurrent problems across the software industry.

In the years since Facebook was started, the number of technology companies has grown rapidly. New companies are born every day, and many adopt tools that Facebook created. React, GraphQL, Cassandra, RocksDB and numerous other pieces of software have emerged from Facebook after being invented and battle-tested under real-world scenarios.

Each of these tools started as a solution to a unique problem within Facebook. Sometimes, Facebook was effectively living in the future, and as the rest of the industry caught up, other companies saw how the tools worked and adopted them for their own use cases.

# FRONTEND

*"The 10-year vision of React is to enable every single engineer who learns this paradigm to be capable of building a user interface for any platform: mobile, desktop, virtual reality, or anything else."*

—TOM OCCHINO, FACEBOOK ENGINEERING DIRECTOR

Back in 2010, frontend web development was a difficult skill to master.

The average website frontend was cobbled together with immature tools like BackboneJS. A large percentage of functionality was handled by JQuery, a Swiss army knife that was used to change the HTML on the page. Web developers were immersed in "callback hell," plagued by the poor networking APIs offered by AJAX.

Today, web applications are powerful and richly interactive. It's easy to forget how quickly things have changed.

Web browsers were not originally used for deeply complex, highly interactive web applications. The web became this way because engineers have repeatedly pushed the frontiers of functionality.

Facebook's early versions were only minimally interactive. Users could post to each other's walls, create friendships, and send messages. The basic abstractions of PHP and AJAX were sufficient to let Facebook developers build the functionality they needed.

As Facebook became popular, the engineers built features that allowed users to engage more rapidly. Newsfeed now updates quickly with new activity from your friends. Messenger has become so popular that Facebook has made the product into its own app. Facebook Groups has evolved from a rigid bulletin board to a vibrant, dynamic chat room.

Facebook was the first highly transactional multi-user consumer application to hit massive scale.

Facebook engineers have said that they borrow many of their engineering ideas from multi-user gaming. Games such as Everquest and World of Warcraft paved the way for the best practices of data flow and frontend rendering that Facebook has employed.

Before Facebook, there was Amazon and Google.

These companies also hit massive scale by the early 2000s. When Facebook started to scale, Amazon and Google had huge amounts of data, too, but it was not user generated. Amazon could run batch updates to its product catalog. Google could run batch updates to its search index. The bulk of the data on Amazon and Google was created at scheduled times.

A batch updating model leads to a fundamentally different application architecture than Facebook's highly interactive, user-generated system.

Facebook's data model needs to be updated all the time. There are small, transactional writes to the data model happening constantly. These updates need to be received on the backend and pushed out to caching layers, then sent directly to the users on the frontend. For every update to the backend, the frontend needs to react appropriately.

The ideal interactive model for Facebook would feel as real-time as a telephone call. New content should stream in as it is being created by other users. A user should not need to refresh the page in order to see updates to the items on it.

Any given object on a webpage has an inherent hierarchy associated with it. A photo has likes and comments. A comment on a photo has its own likes. These elements of an object are nested within one another. The nesting of objects inside other objects can create a very deep tree of relationships. And a webpage should be able to update quickly, even when a user has interacted with a deeply nested element.

Applications before Facebook had struggled to find the right system for frontend data handling. But for Facebook, it was existential. In every area of the Facebook product, frontend engineers were bumping up against the limitations of their JavaScript tools. The poor tooling led to bugs for the end user.

If you used Facebook between 2009 and 2012, you might remember that Facebook frequently showed the incorrect number of notifications in the upper righthand corner. When you logged into Facebook, you might have a red indicator that you had four unread notifications. But when you clicked on the indicator, you would only see one notification.

This bug persisted for years and is an iconic example of the difficulties that Facebook encountered in getting the entire data model to constantly synchronize and update.

As Facebook neared its IPO, the problem with frontend data consistency became a serious issue. A seasoned Facebook engineer named Jordan Walke was working on a new frontend for the Facebook ads product. This is the page where advertisers create and design their ads and decide who they want to show them to.

Advertisers are the people who pay actual money to Facebook. The users of the Facebook ads frontend are the site's main customers, so it was very important that the advertising page that Jordan was designing would operate correctly. But the high degree of interactivity and complexity in the ads page was causing bugs throughout the user interface. If the product were to ship to production, it would lead to a loss of advertiser trust and a drop in revenue for Facebook.

It was unacceptable that the page of maximal revenue importance was malfunctioning in the time leading up to the IPO. Facebook needed to figure out how to create a smooth experience for the advertisers.

Just as Lee Byron and Nick Schrock had realized with GraphQL, Jordan Walke understood that he was encountering an engineering problem that nobody else in the industry had been existentially threatened by. It would require a new engineering solution from scratch.

Jordan took a step back, evaluated the problem from a distance, and decided that an entirely new system for managing frontend components was needed. Working nights and weekends, Jordan built a library called FaxJS, which focused on declarative logic and reactivity.

Not only did FaxJS solve Jordan's problem and allow him to ship the advertising frontend, other engineers throughout

Facebook saw FaxJS and quickly understood that it was a brilliant model for managing frontend components. FaxJS was the prototype for what eventually became ReactJS.

ReactJS gets its name from the fact that components it defines are automatically updated as new information flows into the system. The components are "reactive." In Jordan's vision, the developer would simply declare how the user interface should respond to new data, and the JavaScript framework would take care of the mutative logic.

The concept is simple, but there is a seemingly bottomless amount of work required to fully realize this ideal of user interface libraries.

Jordan Walke began tinkering with his new JavaScript framework back in 2012. In the eight years since then, React has grown to become an entire division of engineering at Facebook. This division is called the React Group, and it has had more impact on the user interfaces we see every day than perhaps any other group of software engineers in the world.

The React Group is managed by Tom Occhino, a proud evangelist of the paradigm shift that React has brought to the software industry. Tom is thoroughly convincing when it comes to all things related to React, and he makes me strangely excited about the future of user interfaces. If the

React Group sold cars, I would eagerly purchase whatever car Tom suggested to me.

"The industry is shifting towards code that is functional, immutable, and declarative," says Tom. "When your code is declarative and functional, it is easier to reason about concurrent and asynchronous programming. Your code becomes more predictable. Your codebase becomes easier to maintain and more reliable over time."

Declarative code is a type of syntax that describes the logic of a program without describing its control flow. Declarative code can be easier to read and reason about than imperative code. A few examples of declarative code are SQL and HTML. Examples of imperative code include Java and Python.

Tom furrows his brow as he dives deeper into the virtues of declarative programming.

"We're moving away from imperative mutation in the view layer. We're moving away from mutable data structures, into a world of more functional, immutable, declarative paradigms, so that we can have better asynchronous programming. When our code is asynchronous, it can be better optimized for taking advantage of multiple cores on devices as our applications get more sophisticated."

Tom is making a profound observation.

React pushes developers towards pure functions. A pure function is a function with no side effects. The result of a pure function is an entirely new variable, which can replace an old variable. This is the idea of immutable data structures.

When the user interface is composed of immutable objects, every object on the page is guaranteed to be the product of the same consistent data set. Every time a React component is updated, the update is the result of backend data being executed through a series of pure functions resulting in a final outcome. By implementing immutable data structures, developers can use React to avoid a common problem in asynchronous programming: race conditions.

Asynchronous programming has frustrated frontend developers since the early 2000s, when JavaScript programs were prone to a condition known as "callback hell."

In callback hell, a user's web page makes multiple requests to different backend servers at the same time. These backend servers respond and deliver resources at different rates, often causing a webpage to load unpredictably.

"I don't hear anyone talking about callback hell anymore," says Tom Occhino. "When you don't have to think about mutations so much, you feel empowered. You don't get caught in the weeds."

React was born out of Facebook's internal struggles: too many files to manage, a complex data model, eventual consistency, buttons that don't work as expected, unpredictable routing issues, and race conditions.

Facebook is not alone in its struggles. These challenges of frontend engineering are epidemic across the web, and in 2013 Facebook open-sourced ReactJS to see if other companies might also find it useful.

When ReactJS was released to the public, the initial response was lukewarm. Many frontend developers ignored it, assuming it was yet another framework that would provide a clunky abstraction on top of raw JavaScript. To the frontend community, it was unclear why ReactJS was any better than AngularJS or BackboneJS.

Some web developers were aesthetically offended by the design of React.

In its early days, one feature of React that was frequently mocked was an innovative file format called JSX. In JSX, the developer is able to work with both HTML and JavaScript in the same file. The JSX is broken into separate HTML and JavaScript files once it is ready to be rendered for the user. Although JSX looks ugly at first glance, the co-location of two different syntax types in the same file creates a convenient experience for the developer.

A less controversial feature of React was its one-way data binding. One-way data binding is a technique for pushing state changes through the DOM tree. It reduced latency for web pages and simplified the logic frontend developers had to think through in order to construct user interfaces. This was in contrast to the two-way data binding model of AngularJS and BackboneJS, which both suffered from latency.

By 2015, the open source community began warming up to React. In 2016, React became the most popular frontend library for building user interfaces on the web, having over-taken Google's AngularJS.

As React's core ideas became popular, more engineers started taking notice and joining the open-source commu-nity. A pattern emerged of engineers trying React in their personal projects or within their companies and becom-ing so fascinated with the framework that they shifted to working on it full-time. Dan Abramov is one such example.

Dan Abramov is a young, wiry engineer with a clean-cut beard and horn-rimmed glasses. Dan's passion for computers started when he was a young user of Micro-soft PowerPoint. Dan discovered that PowerPoint had a "macros" feature, allowing rudimentary programming similar to what is available in Microsoft Excel. His interest in PowerPoint programming eventually blossomed into a fascination with ideas from functional programming, software principles, and React.

Dan famously co-created Redux in the weeks leading up to a software conference. After he finished his demo on the plane ride to the conference, Dan's presentation caused the entire React community to rethink how data moved through React applications. Facebook took note of Dan's community contribution and quickly hired him as an official member of the React team.

Dan has an unflappable kindness and humility, combined with an intellectual spirit that has earned him a cult following among web developers. His level of outreach and technical contribution have made him a sort of accidental mascot for the React project. Since joining Facebook, Dan has become an intermediary between the company and the growing community of open source contributors.

"New developments in React are primarily driven by the technical needs of Facebook," says Dan. "Because we develop such a wide range of products, we encounter a wide range of engineering problems inside of Facebook. Those problems tend to map to what people want externally as well."

There is a positive feedback loop between Facebook and the open source community. Facebook will build a feature into

React that solves a problem for Facebook. Once that feature is open sourced, other companies will adopt it, supporting the new feature and improving it.

React is a beautiful example of the power of open source software.

The software community trusts React, because Facebook depends so heavily on it. "If we introduce a bug in React, our own application is probably going to break," says Dan Abramov.

React has become a large source of investment for Facebook. The React Group is devoted to building React out further and adding continual improvements, updates, and expansions. New versions of React are continually benchmarked. New test suites are regularly added, to ensure quality.

The React team likes to do experiments and has found creative, elegant solutions that add value to the framework. Dan describes the process by which the team explores new projects. "Each project goes through stages. You start with a hunch. You explore a design. Then you actually start working on it with an internal client."

Facebook has hundreds of internal systems that use React, including ads management, newsfeed, events, photos,

Messenger, and Instagram. The entirety of Facebook.com is built with React. To test new projects within React, the React Group works closely with Facebook teams willing to try experimental new features.

After a new feature is tested successfully on a single internal team, Facebook expands it to other experimental groups before enabling it across the entire company.

"We gradually take on more internal clients until we say, 'Okay, let's just try to use it across Facebook. ' Any team at Facebook can start using it and they give us feedback. Each project goes through these multiple stages, and it gets more and more concrete. But it's important that we start by focusing on a small user base and try to make that user base happy and then gradually expand."

Dan believes that this system of slowly releasing React to internal users leads to healthy, stable open source software. Once a new version of React is proven internally, the React Group publishes it to GitHub and shares it with the open source community. React is part of Dan's identity, and he takes the responsibility seriously.

"It's our job to make sure that those thousands of components actually keep working with every new version," Dan says.

React has raised the profile of Facebook engineering by

placing a large, critical piece of infrastructure in the open. The software ecosystem has latched onto React, and today new engineers learning web development will usually pick React as their frontend UI library. Since the software community has consolidated around React, knowledge sharing for frontend developers has become much simpler.

React has become a tool for software education, a fact of which Tom Occhino is proud. "React has lowered the barrier to getting started with frontend software. Over time, we want to let you build something that is more expressive, more sophisticated, and quicker to build with. If you want to learn the complexities of computer science, you can do so progressively over time. But we want to let you build software now."

React represents the idea that software tools should help developers be successful even if they don't know computer science theory. Tom Occhino laments the fact that so many prospective software engineers are intimidated by university computer science.

"I went to school for computer engineering and the first day lecture hall was just packed. People were standing in the aisles. By the end of the semester, two-thirds of the class had dropped computer science as a major because it was too hard. It does not need to be that hard. With React, we want to lower the barrier to entry for computer science."

The conventional computer science education process places a heavy emphasis on theory over practice. Newer forms of software education such as coding bootcamps and online courses reverse this, prioritizing practice over theory. If someone wants to build an app, they should be able to build an app. The option to learn computer science should come later.

The React Group is also focused on simplifying cross-platform development.

React Native allows the software engineering patterns of React to be used on other platforms, such as native iOS and Android applications. This vision excites Tom Occhino. "Once you learn how to use React, you are empowered with a starting point on any platform that you want to build for. We're a really long way away from this, but React Native is a step in this direction."

React Native allows engineers to build user interface components that use React on mobile platforms. React Native fulfills some of the dreams that originally led Facebook to choose HTML5 for its mobile apps, allowing engineers to move more easily between web, Android, and iOS.

Another long-term goal of React is to dramatically improve performance. React components are high-level objects, and there is plenty of room for improvement in between that high-level representation and the low-level execution environment.

"As of today, we've already sped up React significantly from where it was in the beginning," says Tom. "If React code is running slow today, it's very rare that React itself is the bottleneck. But we can still do better. We can explore optimizing compilation and static analysis and dead code elimination and static extraction of repeated UI."

Because React is open source, an improvement in React can improve frontend performance on websites everywhere.

React code is used across the world. The quality of Internet infrastructure is very different in rural Africa than it is in San Francisco. Tom Occhino suggests that React should ideally be able to adapt to these different environments, so that low bandwidth systems can use React applications more efficiently.

"We struggle with how to deliver a good experience on low-end devices in emerging markets. We're constrained by how long it takes to download, parse, and evaluate JavaScript bundles. We're just starting to scratch the surface."

React started as a well-defined solution to a set of problems Facebook was struggling with. It has grown to be the UI framework of choice for Facebook and for a large swath of developers across the world. With React and GraphQL, Facebook has defined new patterns for handling data flow and application state management.

As manager of the React Group, Tom has overseen more than five years of software improvements. But the React ecosystem still feels young to him. "The React code that people write today looks nothing like the React code that was written five years ago. And I have confidence that there's a ton of runway left."

# FACEBOOK
# MOORE'S LAW

*"Facebook itself runs on Facebook."*

—DAN ABRAMOV

Facebook engineers write lots of software. Some of that software is seen by the end user. Facebook has newsfeed algorithms, Like buttons, and messaging products that we interact with on a daily basis.

Behind the scenes, there are engineers at Facebook working on internal software that is only seen by employees and contractors within the company. Facebook builds its own software for calendars, conference room scheduling, video chat, issue tracking, code reviews, and content moderation.

Today, it would seem like madness for a new company to

build all of this software in-house. The average startup uses a set of off-the-shelf vendors such as Zoom, Google Calendar, GitHub, and Slack. But Facebook was started in 2004, before all of these SaaS tools were available.

Facebook builds its communication and collaboration software internally, and all of that software is tied into employees' Facebook identities. At an average software company, the tools are all disconnected. They do not talk to each other smoothly. When you work at Facebook, your work identity is kept seamlessly consistent across every tool, from video conferencing to code review. The uniformly integrated toolset makes the experience of being a Facebook employee totally unique.

Aside from the identity layer and productivity tools, Facebook also builds internal systems for content moderation.

There is an avalanche of content flowing into Facebook at all times. Videos, photos, comments, messages, and news articles get posted to the site by billions of users. Facebook needs to moderate this content to provide the user with a clean experience, but the degree to which Facebook should moderate the content has become a source of massive debate.

Facebook is continually redefining its content moderation policies to accommodate changing cultural and political preferences. Large engineering teams have formed around building tools for automated and human-curated content moderation. Just beneath the surface of the Facebook experience, there is an army of people sifting through Facebook content that has been flagged for moderation. There are complex workflows involving hundreds of support agents. These support agents interact with users, engineers, and product teams.

Content moderation workflows are all supported by software that is built in-house and customized for Facebook. The custom tooling results in smoother operations and consistent content moderation policies.

When Facebook was started in 2004, there were no SaaS products. Facebook could not use GitHub because GitHub did not exist. Facebook could not use Slack because Slack did not exist. Facebook became accustomed to building higher level tools for collaboration and internal support.

More importantly, Facebook was started before the rise of cloud computing. Today, developers take for granted the simplicity of spinning up remote server infrastructure. Back in 2004, every company needed to find physical server hosting, figure out how to share databases, load balance traffic, and maintain secure infrastructure.

In 2004, software was hard to deploy and hard to scale.

Facebook was forced to do everything without the ease of Amazon Web Services.

Amazon Web Services was started in 2006, and most large companies that were started afterwards are built entirely on cloud computing. This includes Lyft, Dropbox, and Airbnb. Because Facebook was started before AWS, the company was forced to develop a core competency in building and scaling backend server infrastructure.

Facebook has architected its own hardware and purchased its own data centers. Facebook has coded its own transactional databases, container orchestration frameworks, and machine learning tools.

Facebook was the first large-scale social network, and one of the biggest modern software companies built in the pre-cloud infrastructure world. Because of these factors, Facebook has dealt with a distinct set of backend software challenges. This makes the company a weird petri dish of software solutions.

One of the most celebrated projects that helped scale Facebook is called the HipHop Virtual Machine, or HHVM for short. HHVM is a virtual machine built to run PHP code efficiently.

HHVM is an example of how Facebook's unique engineering constraints forced the company to solve a problem that nobody else had needed to solve before: how do you scale the world's most popular PHP application?

Facebook was built in PHP, a server-side language that allows developers to work quickly and productively. PHP is interpreted, which means that every line of code is sequentially compiled down to machine code as the program is executing. This is in contrast to an ahead-of-time compiled language like C++, where the program is turned into binary machine code in a compilation step before execution.

As Facebook grew in popularity, the company needed its large volume of backend PHP code to run faster. Keith Adams was a lead engineer on a series of projects that ultimately led to HHVM. Keith describes the first effort to improve the PHP execution speed: a direct transpilation from PHP to C++ called HPHP.

"PHP is slow. C++ is fast. We wanted to see if you could just port PHP down to C++, maybe you get a fast program out of it." Keith was astonished by how successful this move to ahead-of-time compilation turned out to be. "I still find it heroic that you can take a big complicated PHP program like Facebook and compile it to this completely different domain with a very different set of expectations. You compile it, you link it, you produce a gigantic binary, and that binary ran on port 8080 of Facebook for several years."

Going from PHP to C++ provided huge gains in raw execution speed. But C++ required ahead-of-time compilation: the PHP codebase had to be converted to C++ in one long, synchronous step.

Keith wondered if there was an intermediate approach between the pure interpreted runtime of PHP and the ahead-of-time compilation of C++. In between these two types of execution systems is a runtime called a just-in-time compiler or JIT.

In a JIT compiler, the human-readable code is compiled down into bytecode, an intermediate representation that can be interpreted into machine code "just-in-time." Examples of JIT execution runtimes include the Java Virtual Machine, the C# Common Language Runtime, and the JavaScript V8.

JIT languages provide some of the high-level benefits that come with a purely interpreted language, such as better developer productivity. Also, when a program is in bytecode, engineers can optimize it in real time by doing hot code path analysis.

To experiment with bytecode execution, Keith built a system for running PHP on top of the V8 JavaScript virtual machine. But running PHP on top of V8 used too many resources.

"It was too expensive," says Keith. "The crazy thing about PHP is that it exposes the semantics of reference counting to PHP programs. If you try to make a PHP runtime execute on top of V8, or on top of the JVM or any other JIT runtime, you're going to be dealing with the memory footprint of reference counting on top of the memory footprint of tracing collection. You'll have a multiplicative effect of the overheads that you would normally face in each of these individual runtime environments."

It was not feasible for Keith to simply delegate the execution of PHP to a proven compiler like V8.

PHP is a garbage-collected, reference-counted language. Executing a large PHP program requires the allocation of additional memory in order to trace the execution. The resource consumption would be too high given the memory footprint of PHP reference counting together with the JavaScript bytecode memory management overhead of V8 itself.

Keith still wanted to get Facebook's server infrastructure running on a JIT compiler. After ruling out the easy option of reusing an existing runtime, he decided it was necessary for Facebook to build a new compiler from scratch.

The HipHop Virtual Machine (HHVM) is a just-in-time compiler that serves as an execution engine for PHP. In

HHVM, the PHP code is first transpiled into HHBC, a high-level bytecode format that serves as an intermediate language. This bytecode is dynamically executed by the HHVM. The bytecode execution environment allows Facebook to analyze the code as it runs on the server and to optimize it on the fly.

As improvements were made to the backend PHP infrastructure, software execution became faster across Facebook. The hundreds of backend engineers writing PHP code woke up one day with decreased latency and resource consumption.

HHVM is an example of the continuous improvement of software across the company. This ongoing march towards better, faster infrastructure is colloquially known as "Facebook Moore's Law."

Facebook Moore's Law is an allusion to Moore's Law, which describes the exponential increase in cost efficiency of computer hardware over time. Coined by Gordon Moore, co-founder of Intel, Moore's Law has consistently made our computers faster and more powerful every year.

Facebook Moore's Law describes the phenomenon of Facebook product engineers continually benefiting from the efforts of infrastructure engineers.

Just as every developer in the world benefits from lockstep

improvements in CPU technology, every developer at Facebook benefits from the low-level software improvements that people like Keith Adams make possible.

Throughout Facebook, there are infrastructure teams whose sole mission at the company is to make the code across Facebook run faster and more reliably. The effect of such robust platform engineering is that product engineers are empowered to build products imaginatively, without worrying about whether the servers can handle them.

Facebook invests so heavily in its infrastructure that most product engineers feel like they have effectively infinite resources. As they push the bounds of those resources, the infrastructure engineers respond by improving low-level abstractions such as compilers, databases, and networking protocols.

With so much effort put into the underlying infrastructure, the product teams are able to move faster and more securely. They can try bold experiments, because the infrastructure is built to provide safety nets for these experiments.

Pete Hunt was a product engineer at Facebook who worked on video and photo products. He was the first engineer to move from Facebook to the Instagram team after the photo sharing company was acquired, and he has a deep understanding of how products get built at Facebook.

Pete explains that this symbiotic relationship between product engineers and infrastructure engineers is not present at every software company. "At most tech companies, if you want to spin up a database with terabytes of capacity, you have to go file an infrastructure ticket. Make sure there's enough capacity. Make sure there's an on-call engineer that can handle the scale. As a product engineer at Facebook, that didn't happen to me."

"Every all hands, they would announce that performance improved and costs went down. The backend teams were continuously innovating. Stuff would just get faster and cheaper," says Pete Hunt. "It worked really well, and the product owners like myself benefited from it."

One example of infrastructure improvements positively impacting the entire organization has to do with Facebook Live Video. When the Live Video product launched, the high volume of large video streams strained Facebook's infrastructure, causing latency and video buffering issues. With a high-profile product performing poorly for users, there was pressure on the backend engineers to solve the problem immediately.

Streaming video is a difficult feature to build from scratch, and it took multiple iterations to get it to the necessary quality. Senior leadership reviewed the high-level product metrics every week, until it was clear that the backend infrastructure underlying Live Video was thoroughly polished. There were no buffering issues or loading problems: Live Video was fixed.

Often, it is acceptable to release a new product that is not entirely scalable. If it becomes popular, the backend engineers can figure out how to scale it.

The backend engineers at Facebook are motivated by the idea of enabling new product experiences. They enjoy seeing the quality of their infrastructure compound, quarter after quarter, just like the tick-tock improvements of the normal Moore's Law.

# CONCLUSION

*"In his autobiography, Walmart's founder [Sam Walton] expounds on the principles of discount retailing and discusses his core values of frugality and a bias for action—a willingness to try a lot of things and make many mistakes. [Jeff] Bezos included both in Amazon's corporate values."*

—THE EVERYTHING STORE: JEFF BEZOS AND
THE AGE OF AMAZON, BRAD STONE

In the software industry, every new company learns by studying its predecessors.

The industry evolves as technologists survey the companies that came before and decide what they will copy and what they will do differently. Much of this knowledge transfer happens via books written about these companies. This book has made an effort to capture some of the elements of Facebook that enables the company to build popular software.

We hope that readers of this book have found useful knowledge that they can apply to their own businesses and creative projects.

This book is a case study, not an instruction manual. Facebook was built in a specific time, with a specific set of engineering constraints. You should not copy every aspect of Facebook. You should consider the framework for decision making that made Facebook successful, and try to evaluate your own decisions in light of it.

What is the most important takeaway of this book? Move fast.

"Move fast" is a remedy for market adjustments, technology changes, and cultural stagnation. In order for a company to move fast, the entire company must be oriented around speed.

In the previous chapters, we explored Facebook's approach to moving fast. In this conclusion, we briefly revisit the Facebook story, and consider what we can learn from it.

Facebook is a consumer technology business with a cash cow. The company has very high profit margins on its core business unit of mobile advertising. This ad unit has a zero marginal cost to each individual unit sold. Facebook's cash cow puts the company in such a strong financial position that it is able to take on heavy capital expenses for experiments, top talent, and a luxurious campus.

It is much easier to move fast when a company has a cash cow, a large source of continuous cash flows. A cash cow allows a company to invest aggressively, placing lots of bets and accepting that many will not succeed.

Facebook did not get its cash cow by accident.

Facebook developed its cash cow business model by making a difficult decision to shift its core focus to mobile and adapt its entire engineering force to the post-mobile world. Facebook moved fast at every layer of the organization to reorient itself around native mobile applications.

It was in September 2011 that Facebook realized it needed to focus all of its resources on mobile. By October 2013, Facebook could comfortably say that it had built a mobile advertising cash cow. In those two years, the company pivoted completely to mobile. Moving fast allowed Facebook to execute this pivot.

If Facebook had not moved fast, it might still be a company based around desktop advertising, struggling to keep up with the changing consumer trends.

A software company without a cash cow should be oriented

around finding one. Only by building a cash cow can a company break away from the brutal competition that comes from mediocre cash flows. Moving fast can help a company develop a cash cow. Once a company has strong cash flows, it can use the cash to move even faster.

The most powerful software companies build their cash cow business models by moving fast and being ruthlessly decisive.

After mobile became profitable, Facebook decisively abandoned its large acquisition of the cloud services company Parse and drove even harder towards mobile advertising. Facebook was equally decisive in its response to Google+, quickly rallying the employees to come in on weekends.

Facebook is able to move fast because it has a cohesive company culture. A cohesive company culture is only possible if the employees enjoy working at the company. Employees only enjoy working at a company if they feel their work is individually rewarding.

It may seem paradoxical, but at Facebook, individualism drives social cohesion.

Every company can do this at some level. Every company can give engineers the opportunity to express themselves creatively. By encouraging engineers to try new things, a company earns the trust of its employees. Treating employees as creative individuals helps with social health across the company. A creative engineering environment can give rise to unexpected products and solutions.

When engineers are trusted to make creative decisions, they feel empowered by the company. They are more likely to work together.

Facebook's bootcamp program sets up a healthy relationship between the company and the employees from day one. Bootcamp allows employees to determine what to work on based on their interests and the needs of the overall organization. When new employees are given a choice of what to work on, they are more likely to dive into their project with enthusiasm.

Facebook employees are encouraged to find work that is enjoyable and fulfilling. Their work must also serve the company. There is one word that every Facebook employee knows: impact.

An employee can be extremely creative, but if their creativity does not lead to business success, they will not be rewarded. When evaluating an employee during a performance review, management should always consider one key question: is this employee having measurable positive impact?

A Facebook employee should always be able to explain their impact on the company. In a performance review, "impact" can be the sole metric that implies success or failure. And for engineers, the most definitive way to show impact is by writing code. Code wins arguments.

The focus on impact helps Facebook refine the squishy, psychologically cushioned existence that comes from such a comfortable working life. Yes, Facebook has lots of perks. Yes, the work can be very fun and individually rewarding. But if you can't show measurable impact, you will lose your job.

Employee freedom drives Facebook to spontaneously build creative new technologies. A focus on impact hones that creative energy into something meaningful. And the large cash flows ensure that this engine of creative productivity has room to thrive and explore lots of different areas.

The combination of experimentation, strong talent, and plentiful resources puts Facebook in rarified business territory. As a result, the engineering department at Facebook is like an alien civilization.

It is worth trying to understand what makes these aliens successful, even if it doesn't make sense to copy their actions directly.

Facebook's engineering stack reflects the company's DNA.

Facebook started as a PHP application and has built elaborate PHP infrastructure to support it. Scaling PHP allowed Facebook to double down on the technology that made it successful, even if PHP has historically been ridiculed.

Facebook's pivot to mobile created the need for new release engineering tools and the networking middleware GraphQL. By building strong mobile tooling, Facebook was able to reinforce its identity a mobile-enabled social networking company.

There are countless technologies that Facebook has developed that are not covered in this book. If you are looking to understand how Facebook builds software, the individual technologies are less important to consider than the overall philosophy around innovation and software management.

Facebook's backend engineering teams work to support fast product development led by product engineering teams. This stark division of labor between backend engineering and product engineering was historically very expensive. It used to cost a lot of money to have a dedicated backend engineering department. But cloud computing has changed the economics that drive today's structure of software teams.

Across the software industry, the practice of well-defined backend teams supporting user-focused product development has become known as "platform engineering." Many newer companies have a small platform engineering team that standardizes the infrastructure deployed throughout the organization.

The most dramatic shift in software that has occurred in the last ten years is the maturity of cloud computing.

One of the downstream impacts of cloud computing is the rise of platform engineering. A platform engineering team defines the software platform that other teams in the organization build on top of.

Facebook needed to build its own platform. Today, a company can buy its own platform, stitching together its ideal software stack with a custom blend of paid infrastructure and open source tools.

Whereas Facebook's platform engineering team requires the work of hundreds of engineers writing custom code, a newer company today can succeed with a small team of platform engineers who buy software from vendors such as Amazon Web Services.

A platform engineering team chooses tools for cloud infrastructure, containerization, virtualization, continuous integration, feature flagging, databases, queueing, data infrastructure, service mesh, load balancing, and more. In each of these software categories, there are multiple vendors selling high-quality products.

A new product company can choose how to construct its platform out of cloud infrastructure and high-level software-as-a-service products. There is also a wealth of free open source software that companies across the industry build together, providing a massive public good.

The growth of cloud infrastructure has mostly settled the long-standing debate of "build versus buy." In order to move fast, a new company should choose "buy." Although Facebook succeeded by building its internal software stack from the ground up, a company being built today should probably not create as much software from scratch as Facebook has.

Facebook was built by rethinking best practices. "Best practices" represent the proven methodologies for product development, management, and software engineering. Facebook has questioned the dogmas around how software can and should be built.

Every company should be rethinking best practices because the world is changing faster than ever before. Products such as GitHub, Amazon Web Services, and Slack have each transformed the possibilities for how companies can be built.

In Facebook's case, "rethinking best practices" was applied to how new software is built. Newer companies will be rethinking best practices in light of how software is bought, used, and combined. Modern technology trends such as functions-as-a-service and "low-code" tools have the potential to upend the best practices of software development to the same extent that Amazon Web Services did.

The companies that adopt new products early learn how to use them fastest. Aggressively adopting new technologies allows a company to see what kinds of old best practices have become outmoded because of the emergence of something new.

This is what makes the software industry so exciting. Software is the continuous layering of new abstractions on top of old ones. Every new generation of software is built on top of the abstractions of the previous generation.

The same generational development occurs at the level of strategy. Every new generation of companies builds on the strategic learnings of the previous generations. Company strategy is often defined by the leader, but it can only be carried out by the employees, and every employee plays a part in bringing that strategy to life.

This book has been a high-level overview of how Facebook builds software. Now that you are at the end of the book, you may be asking yourself whether this was a useful reading exercise. You could have spent this time practicing a new programming language or reading about how machine learning works.

Through this book, we tried to present Facebook through the lens of software company strategy. And we hope these lessons of strategy are useful as you proceed in your career, whether you are an engineer, a manager, an investor, or a student.

Facebook pivoted to mobile, developed an advertising cash cow, fostered a culture of systematic innovation, and invented thousands of new technologies along the way. None of this was an accident. None of this would have been possible without a relentless, deliberate focus on the overarching strategy of the company.

Wherever you are in your software career, it is worth studying companies' operational strategies. It is worth understanding how strategy affects every layer of an organization.

Once you understand company strategy, you can determine how to have a higher impact within your own organization. You can decide whether your company would benefit from moving faster. You can decide that the leader of your company is a poor strategist and leave the company.

If you study enough different strategies, you will inevitably figure out a strategy of your own. You will see an opportunity for your own company to start. And you will know how to implement that strategy from start to finish, from product to culture to technology.

# ACKNOWLEDGEMENTS

Thanks to Pete Hunt and Nick Schrock for spurring this project to happen, and to all the current and former Facebook employees who came on *Software Daily* for interviews: Dhruba Borthakur, Lee Byron, Keith Adams, Tom Occhino, Pedram Keyani, Kent Beck, Chuck Rossi, Dan Abramov, Charity Majors, Raylene Yung, Ilya Sukhar, Mike Vernal, Jocelyn Goldfein, Jeff Rothschild, Peter Deng, Arturo Bejar, Venkat Venkataramani, and Antonio Garcia Martinez.

My family: Dad, Mom, Margo, Haskell, Joel, Leanne, Michael—your support means the world to me.

Erika Hokanson was instrumental in supporting the logistics of *Software Daily* as we worked on this project. Thanks to Pranay Mohan for setting sail on this journey with me in the early days of the podcast. Robert Blumen is the godfather of software podcasting, and without his guidance I would not be where I am.

My mentors and friends: Mike Scott, Melinda Darrow, Jennifer Li, Haseeb Qureshi, Auren Hoffman, Patrick Mathieson, Jonathan Brill, Owen Davis, William Gruger, Austin Hambrick, Konstantine Buehler, Lan Ho, Joseph Jacks, Charlotte Kwon, Winston Lee, Burt Jones, Andrew Gray.

Thanks to Hal and Tucker and the team at Scribe Media for making this process so easy.

Finally, the listeners of *Software Daily* have supported us through all the different experiments we have tried in our five-year journey. I hope this one paid off and that the end product is enjoyable to read.

# ABOUT THE AUTHOR

**JEFF MEYERSON** is the host of *Software Daily*, a podcast about engineering and software strategy. Over the last five years, *Software Daily* has featured more than 1,000 interviews with engineers, CEOs, managers, investors, and industry analysts. Meyerson has worked as a software engineer at several companies, including Amazon. He's an investor in software companies targeted at developers. He writes music as The Prion, and you can find him on Spotify.

CPSIA information can be obtained
at www.ICGtesting.com
Printed in the USA
FSHW011728020721
82922FS